pigeon racing

pigeon racing

By Dr. Herbert R. Axelrod
& Edwin C. Welty

With diagrams by Edwin C. Welty

 STERLING PUBLISHING CO., INC.   NEW YORK

Oak Tree Press Co., *Ltd.* London & Sydney

OTHER BOOKS OF INTEREST

Bird Life (For Young People)
Cage Bird Identifier
How to Raise and Train Pigeons

Acknowledgments

The publisher would like to thank the following for the use of some of the photographs in this book: L. Kovacs for photo on p. 89 (cock owned by L. Kovacs); R. Dinkfelt for photos on p. 145 (foundation stock owned by R. Dinkfelt); Lilo Hess for photo on p. 102; Orlando from Three Lions for photos on pp. 6, 55, 61, 68, 92, 122, 124, 134, 175; TFH Publications for many photos on racing-training techniques used throughout the book; E. Topoleski for photos on pp. 36 (cock owned by P. Veegaete, Fraser, Mich.), 38 (cock via V. De Feyter), 39, 41, 52 (hen via V. De Feyter), 53 (cock bred by Dr. L. F. Whitney), 82, 86 (cock bred and owned by E. Topoleski), 131, 162 (hen bred by G. Shilton, North Haledon, N.J.), 195 (hen bred and owned by E. Topoleski); U.S. Air Force for photos on pp. 2 and 14; Louise Van der Meid for photos on pp. 29, 43, 46, 47, 52, 65, 66, 67, 90, 106, 159, 171, 179; Van Wonterghem (Kuurne, Belgium) for photos on pp. 126, 127, 136, 137, 152, 153 (these long-distance birds owned by G. and M. Vanhee, Wervik, Belgium), p. 157 (hen owned by Jules Galles, Meulebeke, Belgium); E. C. Welty for the map on p. 108, the diagrams on pages 18, 19, 58, 74, 75, 76, 165, 181, 186, 192 and for the photos on pp. 22 (loft owned by the Duez Brothers, Jeanette, Pa.), 23, 24, 25 (top loft owned by A. Lacivita, E. McKeesport, Pa.), 27, 28, 70 (hen bred and owned by E. C. Welty), 78, 79, 83 (cock bred by R. P. Fike), 84, 115, 117 (both hens owned by A. Lacivita), 128 (hen bred and owned by T. Bocek, North Versailles, Pa.— bottom loft on p. 24 also owned by T. Bocek), 129, 144 (loft owned by R. Dinkfelt, West Miflin, Pa.), 198 (birds owned by E. C. Welty).

CONTENTS

Stall traps like this are the most popular in the United States, while European flyers generally clock their birds in the nest box. Whether you use the natural or widowhood systems your bird must be trained not to linger on the loft roof. Remember, your pigeon already has the homing ability—and this book will help you to develop it.

One advantage of belonging to a club is that members co-operate in arranging van-tosses—and with this type of training your young flyers easily learn what racing conditions are like and how to find the way home without the aid of a loft mate.

INTRODUCTION

Pigeon racing is one of the great sports in which animals compete against one another. While dog racing and horse racing are sports of the wealthy and victories are directly related to the amount of money spent for trainers, training and blood-lines, quite the contrary is true of pigeon racing. The trainers are almost always the owners; the training is done by these same dedicated owners; and there is almost no existing blood-line of pigeon which consistently provides victories for both the breeders and the fancier who buys his stock.

Racing pigeons respond to proper training and care, and like any other athletic undertaking, the more strictly the proven principles of pigeon racing are adhered to, the more successful the pigeons will be in competition. There is almost no "art" left in pigeon racing; it is almost pure science.

This book is the result of my keeping and racing pigeons for almost 35 years. I have tried all techniques and visited pigeon lofts all over the world. His majesty, King Leopold III of Belgium, has assisted me in combing Belgium for the best racing pigeons; other people, not so famous, but just as nice, have gotten me the best birds from South Africa and Holland, as well as from Scotland where pigeon racing is almost a national sport. All pigeons respond to training and care and are equal, but not better than, the best birds available for a day's pay anywhere else in the world.

Much of what I am writing has never before been published, since these were the "trade secrets" of the French and American Intelligence agencies that trained pigeons for carrying important "classified" documents.

I do not race pigeons any more, so I can tell the whole technique without holding anything back. Just follow my suggestions step by step and compare them with any other advice that you may have been given. I am sure you will have little trouble in being consistently among the top winners.

Dr. Herbert R. Axelrod

For 22 years the sport of pigeon racing has been a large part of my life, and it is really hard to put into words what pigeons mean to me. Pigeon racing gets into your blood, and I find it impossible to do without racing pigeons. The pigeon has meant many things to me, and most of them have been good. Perhaps no other bird in the world has done as much for Man as the pigeon.

I must honestly say that the pigeon loves Man and may very well be Man's best animal friend.

With this I dedicate my part of this book to the pigeon itself.

Edwin C. Welty

Here, a good blue-bar. Because blue pigeons greatly outnumber red pigeons, it seems that the blues win most of the races. It is a misconception, however, that red coloration automatically makes a pigeon an inferior racer.

I. THE PIGEON'S HISTORY

Nobody knows exactly when Man first used the pigeon to carry messages. There is evidence that as far back as 3,700 years ago, Man discovered the homing ability of pigeons. In ancient sieges, pigeons were used to carry messages about troop movements, while the spies within the besieged cities used pigeons to keep themselves informed about what was going on outside the city walls. Julius Caesar used pigeons in many of his war campaigns. Experts on prehistoric remains have provided us with proof of the high regard that ancient peoples held for the pigeon. Archeologists have found inscriptional records that the pigeon and the dove occupied a position of reverence and were regarded as holy in early civilizations. The earliest known record of domesticated pigeons dates back to the 5th Egyptian Dynasty (about 3000 B.C.). And in the 18th Dynasty, Thothmes III made mention of "258 pairs of pigeons and 5,237 pigeons of another kind."

Pigeons and doves are mentioned in the mythology of almost every religion known. In the old Middle Eastern religions, this bird was sacred to Astarte, the goddess of love. Pigeons, doves, and turtledoves were mentioned in the Old Testament as the only birds allowed under the Law of Moses to be sacrificed in early Hebrew rituals of purification.

Leviticus 14: 21–22: "And if he be poor and cannot get so much; then he shall take . . . And two turtledoves, or two young pigeons, such as he is able to get; and the one should be a sin offering, and the other a burnt offering."

Also, in the Christian religion the dove is emblematic of the Holy Spirit.

Matthew 3: 16: ". . . and Jesus, when He was baptized, went up straightway out of the water; and, lo, the heavens were opened unto him, and He saw the Spirit of God descending like a dove, and lighting upon him."

All through the annals of time the pigeon has played a large part in the history of Man. Even wars demanded the services of the pigeon. Sending messages by pigeon has long been known to military men as one of the most effective means of communication. Not only did the ancient armies use the pigeon for communication but so, too, did the armies engaged in World

Besides performing tasks in ancient civilizations, the pigeon (dove) has played a part in mankind's spiritual beliefs from Astarte-worship to the Judeo-Christian religions.

Military training tosses like this one from a portable combat loft made possible feats like that of Cher Ami.

War I, World War II, and the Korean conflict. Nobody will ever know how many lives were saved by message-carrying pigeons, but one thing is known for sure: that history pages would have been written very differently if it had not been for pigeons.

Many pigeons have gone down in history as being war heroes. Many men owe their lives to these pigeons. The best known of these war-hero pigeons was Cher Ami. On October 27, 1918, an American battalion fighting on the Verdun front advanced too far into German-held territory, and the men found themselves surrounded. Every means of communication with the rest of the American fighting force was gone. Several pigeons were released, but were unable to get through. Finally Cher Ami rose to the sky, only to be hit by shrapnel. Even with severe wounds, he flew for 25 minutes to return home to 77th division headquarters and save the "Lost Battalion."*

Even while such history was being made, the fact remains that deeds like this would have been impossible if it were not for the pigeon hobbyist. Pigeons are kept by people from every walk of life. It may be the rich man on the hill or the poor man down the street, but whoever it is, you know that they are dedicated and love their birds.

Queen Victoria kept Jacobins; Mary Queen of Scots kept Barbs; Elizabeth Barrett Browning kept doves; King George V and Roy Rogers kept racing pigeons. Even though there are hundreds of varieties of pigeons, none is held in such high esteem as the racing pigeon.

Our modern racing pigeon is a breed of recent creation, with Belgium and England given credit for its development. Today's racing pigeon is a cross of many different breeds. It is a mixture of the Eastern Carrier, the Owl, the Dragoon, the Horseman, the Chesturlet and the Camus. The Belgians are given credit for starting the sport of pigeon racing. The first pigeon races on record were held in the early part of the 19th century in Belgium. Today it is the national sport there, with some 220,000 participants. The world population of racing pigeon enthusiasts is estimated at seven and one half million. The sport of racing pigeons started in the United States at the same time it started in England (1871). Today there are approximately 50,000 racing-pigeon flyers in the United States.

During the 1890's American interest in racing pigeons increased and spread into all the larger cities on the Eastern Seaboard. In June of 1896, 570 birds competed in a 500-mile race, with 35 homing the same day. This race proved that the sport of pigeon racing was in America to stay.

*As a result of this service to the U.S. army, Cher Ami was mounted after death and is still on display in the Smithsonian Institution, Washington, D.C. The Lost Battalion was a group of soldiers from New York, commanded by Major Charles S. Whittlesey.

2. THE LOFT

One of the most important factors in being a top pigeon-flyer is the loft you provide for your pigeons. Every successful pigeon-flyer has a loft that is properly constructed. The actual cost of construction has no bearing on the amount of success obtained.

Planning the Loft

This chapter will guide you in the proper way to construct your pigeon loft. It is surprising that the design of the loft is all too often neglected. If you live in an area where the houses are close together, a loft must be constructed that will fit in accordingly. It should be neatly constructed, so no one has reason to complain about its appearance. Build your loft so that it faces *away* from the direction in which bad weather prevails. It is impossible to condition a pigeon that lives in a cold, damp loft. Try to build the loft in a quiet spot and far enough from nearby houses so that people won't complain about noise. Also try to keep it away from high-tension wires because the birds may meet with an accident.

Before you begin to draw your plans, take time out to visit as many lofts as possible and take notes and pictures. Once you have a general knowledge, then draw your plans. Before you begin construction, you should check local building codes and ordinances.

To tell you how to build the ideal loft is somewhat complex. For a loft built in the Chicago area would not work for the fancier in Florida or Liverpool. Therefore this chapter just gives a general idea on building a loft. You must improvise according to your locality.

Loft size is very important. You should plan on three partitions: one for breeders, one for young birds, and one for old birds [birds that have reached at least their second year of flying]. Do not let the height of the partitions be so high that pigeons can fly over your head. Partition *sizes* may vary according to the amount of birds you want to keep. Still, an ideal size is when you are able to touch all four walls when standing in the middle of a single partition. If at all possible, build a hallway into your loft. This will .give you plenty of storage space, and it allows each section to have its own entrance.

Foundation and Floor

Many kinds of building materials will suit the purpose, but timber is the best. The foundation should consist of seven block pillars, each 18″ high and square. Place one in each corner of the loft; then one in the middle front, one in the middle back, and one directly in the middle of the floor. This will leave a space under the loft high enough so that cats, mice, rats and other pests cannot hide without being seen. Also, it enables air to circulate under the loft, thus keeping it *dry*. On top of the pillars, build the framework for the floor. Lay the flooring so that the grain of the wood runs in the same direction that you will be cleaning the loft. This prevents splintering of the floor. Before laying the floor, creosote the framework and the underside of the floorboards. Creosote is a heavy oily liquid distilled from wood tar. It preserves wood and will prevent your loft floor from being infested by insects.

The Roof

Keep the following rules in mind when you are building the loft roof, regardless of what style you choose. The pitch of the roof should run from front to back. This allows the rain to run

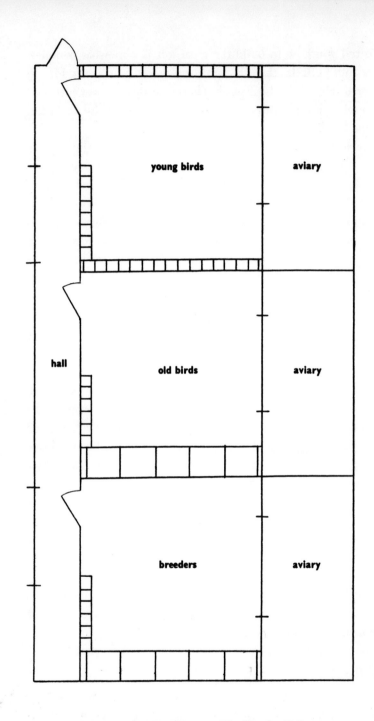

FLOOR PLAN

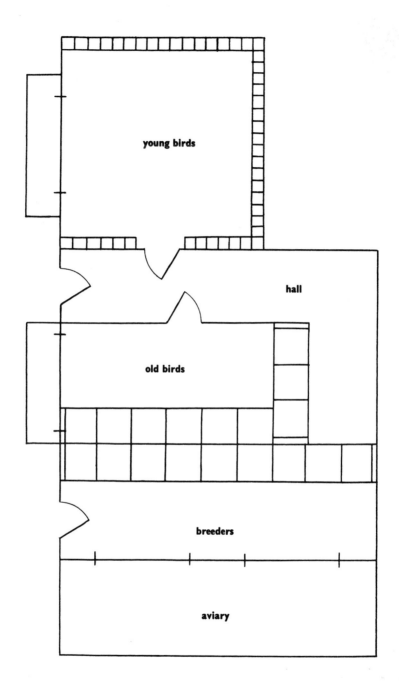

FLOOR PLAN

An ideal set-up for skylights. Note the picket fence that discourages the racers from landing on the roof.

to the back and makes it less tempting for the birds to land on. A 1-foot overhang on all four sides is advisable. Use good-grade roofing material and make sure that the roofing nails do not protrude into the loft's ceiling. A small picket fence should be attached to the front edge of the roof. This discourages the birds from landing on the roof and it also makes it easier to train them to land only on the landing board. Skylights are very beneficial to the health of the pigeon. A bright, warm, dry loft means health and success. The importance of a bright and dry loft cannot be stressed enough.

The Sides

If you plan on an inner wall, the placement of the studs is not too important. If there is only an outer wall, space the studs so

Your loft need not be as elegant as this, but all lofts should abound in sunshine and fresh air.

that the perches and nest boxes fit between them. The sides and back of the loft should be without windows: this is where the doors, perches, and nest boxes belong. Construct the

Another loft ensuring that the pigeon will not lack sunlight and air— this one built on top of a tall city building.

Always make the landing board waist-high to ensure yourself maximum control of your birds. Note, too, the roof overhang and large skylights of this loft.

windows in the hall in such a way that rain cannot enter when they are opened. The front of the loft is where the windows, traps, and landing board belong. The landing board should be as large as possible. Two feet wide by the length of your loft is ideal. Cover it with a heavy roofing material, making sure that dampness cannot warp it. The height of the landing board is very important. It is advisable to have it waist-high. This allows you complete control of the birds when trapping. In the United States the stall traps are the most popular, while in the European countries, the birds are trained to fly through a window or door and are then clocked in their nests.

The dimensions for making stall traps should be taken from the loft that you feel has the best trapping system. Use the best grade wood possible; the bobbs should be made of aluminum. Take your time: do not rush and make needless mistakes.

The windows should be as large as possible, so that plenty of fresh air and sunshine enter the loft. Hang the windows in such a way that, when they are opened, the pigeons are unable to perch on them. Some type of wire or dial framing should be made for the front of each window. Such meshing prevents anything from entering or leaving when the windows are open.

Ventilation

You may have just completed the most beautiful loft, but if you do not have proper ventilation, forget about being a success. Pigeons need plenty of clean fresh air, and when this is not available many problems develop. You achieve good ventilation when "bad" air is replaced with fresh air without causing an air current to blow directly on your pigeons. Make all the partitions completely solid, even the partition doors. Small metal ventilators may be installed next to the floor at the front of the loft. In addition, roof vents should be installed, which allow the stale air to leave. Make sure you install roof vents in such a way that it is impossible for strong air currents to blow directly down on your pigeons.

Good ventilation is one of the most important items in obtaining good health. In fact, you may have to change your ventilation system many times before you find the correct system for your loft.

If you get a heavy pigeon smell upon entering the loft, you know that there is poor ventilation. On the other hand, check

Small ventilators installed at floor level in the loft ensure that these birds will enjoy proper ventilation.

A garage-top loft equipped with roof vents. Note the pleasant appearance of this loft.

for harmful air currents at night. There is no way that a pigeon can be brought into racing form if he is subjected to harsh air currents.

Aviaries (Flypens)

Aviaries are a very essential part of any loft. This is another item that is too often neglected. Aviaries allow the pigeons to

A pitched roof with the prescribed 1-foot overhang characterizes this attractive racing loft. The owner is an acknowledged champion.

This loft's aviaries are ideal. The landing board and stall traps are on the other side of the loft.

A perfect aviary. Boards running the entire length of the flypen give the pigeons ample perching space while the covered over roof permits use in bad weather.

This fancier has built separate aviaries for his breeders and racers, even though you might think that roof-top space is scarce in a city or large town. The landing board and stall traps are on the top of the aviaries.

have a constant supply of fresh air and sunshine, and the aviary is specially important to the breeders as an exercising pen, because these birds cannot be liberated. Instead of giving the flyers open-loft, you can leave them in the aviary to rest and soak up plenty of sunshine.

The breeders' aviary should be as large as possible, while the flyers' may be smaller. The aviary may consist of a wooden framework made with 2×2 planks or 2×4's and can be meshed with $1'' \times 2''$ galvanized wire. The floor should be $1'' \times 1''$ galvanized wire. This makes it much easier for the pigeons to walk on. It is advisable to have a solid roof, thus allowing the pigeons to use the aviary in bad weather. Inside the aviary, provide plenty of perches for the birds to sit on. Ideal perches are $1'' \times 4''$ boards running the entire length of the aviary. There should be at least a $\frac{1}{2}''$ space between the perch and the wire. This allows for easier cleaning and provides less chance of the birds' damaging their feathers. Baths can be given in the aviary, but do not keep any food or water in it because there are too many chances of contamination. At least once a month the ground under the aviary should be raked. Right after you do this, add sand, lime, or new earth. All aviaries should have a door for your convenience in cleaning and giving the all-important bath.

Inside the Loft

Keep in mind when building your loft that there should be as few cracks and corners as possible in which insects and parasites can hide. The hall is a good storage area. Build shelves so that everything can be kept neat, clean, and convenient. Keep the feed in an area where it is impossible to get any dampness. (See Chapter 5 on Feeding.)

There are many different types of perches and nest boxes. The ones described in the following paragraphs are the most

Dangerous amounts of dirt have accumulated here because the perches were constructed to fit flush against the wall. The owner of these birds should have ensured their health by building the perches 1 inch out from the wall.

popular. Do not use plywood in making perches or nest boxes, because it splinters and causes damage to flight feathers. Make all the nest boxes and perches removable. This will make cleaning and maintenance easier.

The young-bird partition consists of only perches. They should run from the ceiling to about *2 feet from the floor*. It is a natural instinct for pigeons to perch high, and when a pigeon is forced to perch low, it is not content. Always have more perches than birds. There is nothing more cruel than a bird's being forced to perch on the floor or on a feeder.

The box-perch is the most popular and should be made to fit between the wall studs. If the wall studs are spaced 24″ apart, the outer dimensions of the box should be 24″ × 50″. The boards the pigeons perch on should be 3″ wide or wider. The

In this loft the perches are built away from the wall. The blue-bar splash cock shown here will be in better form thanks to this construction.

This fancier has been careful to see that his pigeons have large enough nest boxes. Never stint your birds on nesting space! (Ideal dimensions are given in the text.)

two outer boards forming part of the box and the middle board should be 1″ wider than the perches themselves. The reason for this is: whenever such boards are set into the wall, there is an inch gap behind the perch. This makes cleaning easier and prevents the birds from pecking at one another from behind the perch. Space the perches 10″ apart. When complete, this will give you ten perches, each measuring 10″ × 12″. Plane or file the sharp edge off the front of each perch to prevent damage to the pigeons' breast-bones.

The size of the nest boxes depends on how large the partitions are. The nest boxes need not conform to any set rules, but must be large enough for the birds' comfort. The size may be cut down depending on the space you have available. The flyers' section will have two or three times as many nests as the breeders'. An ideal nest box size is 24″ wide, 16″ deep, and 18″ high. Try to keep the breeders' nests at these dimensions—the flyers' nests can be much smaller. (See Chapters 11 and 13 on Racing.) The dimensions just given will allow the breeders to tread right in the nest, and there is still enough room for two nest bowls. The front of the nest boxes should be made separate from the nest. A removable nest-box front will allow you easy

A properly constructed nest box. The door, when open, should be able to serve as a perch.

This inexpensive racing loft was once a chicken house. At very little cost the owner made it over into three compartments: flyers', breeders', and young birds'.

cleaning. There are many different designs for the fronts of the nest boxes. One type having much to recommend it is the nest front that is made out of dowels or laths $1'' \times 2''$. This is attached to the nest box by means of a bracket and, when placed to the front of the framework, gives the nest a cagelike effect. The dowels or laths making up the front of the nest box have a small opening on either the left or right. This opening is covered by a door hinged on the lower side, so that when it is opened it serves as a perch for birds entering the nest. When making the fronts, do not put all the entrances on one side but alternate them from left to right. This reduces the chance of a pigeon's entering the wrong nest. *Do not build the nests flush with the floor*, but have them at least $3''$ above the floor. This allows for air circulation and also a hiding place for youngsters that fall out of the nest. (Very often when youngsters fall out of their nests, an overly aggressive pigeon will attack such a youngster—frequently harming it or even killing it.)

One little reminder is to paint the outside of the loft and keep it clean and neat, so the people next door to you do not have anything to complain about. There is nothing worse than seeing an unkept loft both inside and out. Keep the loft in such a condition that you are not ashamed to show it at any time.

This chapter has given you the most important points in building a loft. A subject as important as this could very well be made into a book by itself. So remember when building: take your time and build the loft right. If questions arise, do not be afraid to ask for help. Remember: When you are keeping pigeons, mistakes are hard to correct.

3. KEEPING THE LOFT CLEAN

Much has been said about keeping the loft clean. This is so important that the subject is well worth an entire chapter. Most pigeon fanciers recognize the importance of proper sanitation, but nevertheless you would be surprised at the number of flyers who neglect this all-important matter. Some lofts are kept in such a filthy state that proper health of the inhabitants is next to impossible. Some birds are so infested with lice and mites that it would be impossible to count them. Year after year the owners of these same pigeons keep dreaming of one day becoming a champion. The fact is that their laziness will prevent them from ever fulfilling their dreams.

There are many ways to keep the floor clean. The most common practice is to scrape the floor with some sort of flat-edged metal scraper. Some fanciers scrape the floor as often as twice a day. If time permits, this is ideal, but very few fanciers have this much time. In most lofts, twice a week seems to be the common practice.

The frequency with which your loft needs cleaning is really determined by the amount of birds kept. If you keep a large number of birds, the loft floor will be dirty in a matter of hours.

Before scraping the floor, sprinkle it with a diluted solution of a pine-scented disinfectant. This helps in killing germs, gives the loft a sweet aroma, and keeps down the dust. Always scrape *with* the grain of wood and in one direction. This helps eliminate splinters and it teaches your pigeons that there is a certain consistency to the cleaning habit, thus eliminating wildness during the cleaning process.

About once a week, or on very damp days, sprinkle a little powdered carbola on the floor. This prepared whitewash serves as a preventative against insects and parasites. (You can buy it easily in most feed stores.)

Many fanciers use sand on their loft floors. This is called the litter or deep-litter system. More fanciers are going to this system every year in search of new ideas to improve the health of their birds. Many have found that the deep-litter system works very well and would never go back to the daily drudgery of scraping the floors.

With the litter system, a covering of between $\frac{1}{2}''$ to $2''$ of washed, coarse river-bottom sand is spread evenly on the loft floor. A $2''$ strip is nailed to the doorways to prevent the sand from spreading into unwanted areas. A little lime or carbola may be mixed with the sand.

The droppings will form a type of mat on top of the sand. A fine-toothed rake is drawn very lightly over the surface, and this removes the droppings. Rake the floor as often as possible because you still do not want a build-up of droppings and at least twice a month, sift the sand through fine wire to eliminate dirt or droppings that were not picked up by the raking. After sifting, add a little more carbola or lime, making sure it is spread evenly throughout the sand. Change the sand as often as you feel is necessary.

At least once a year the floor should be painted with a fine-grade creosote. Do not use anything but the finest grade available because if you use heavy creosote it will never dry. Do not put the birds back into their partitions until the floor is completely dry. There is nothing sadder than seeing a team of birds with creosote on their feathers.

The fanciers who use sand maintain that there is a tendency for pigeons to incur less sickness in the course of the year.

Before you clean the floor, scrape all the perches. At least once every two weeks, put roost paint on the perches as a preventative against lice and mites.

During breeding season take special care to keep the nest boxes clean. Every time you clean the floor, scrape the droppings from the nest boxes. When youngsters are in the nest keep the nests spotlessly clean. Do not let the nesting material become too dirty. It is a good policy to change the nesting material at least once before the bird is weaned (when the squabs are two weeks old is a good time for the first changing). It does not hurt to sprinkle a little carbola, lime, or roost paint in the nest after cleaning.

When the hen is about to lay her second round, give her a clean nest bowl. The dirty nest bowl should be scrubbed with a strong disinfectant and left to dry in the sun. The bottoms of wooden nest bowls may be painted with a fine-grade creosote. Once a year scrub the nest boxes with a strong disinfectant and either paint or whitewash them.

Twice a year, during off season, the entire loft should be scrubbed with a strong disinfectant or lye, to eliminate any mould or bacteria build-up. (While floor scraping, the application of carbola and the like are year-round routines, you should do the thorough disinfecting with lye only during the off season so as not to overexcite the birds.)

At least once every two years whitewash the inside of the loft with either carbola or lime. Do not use an overabundance of lime because it has a tendency to dry out feathers.

For the sake of the people who live near you, do not neglect the outside of the loft. Areas of ground that the birds frequent the most should be raked; and sand, lime, or fresh dirt should be added to sweeten the earth. During moulting season you will find many feathers outside the loft. These should be picked up so that winds do not carry them into adjacent yards.

Do not let the outside of the loft become too shabby. Paint it when needed to keep it neat and clean, giving it an appearance of health and sanitation.

AU 61 RMC 1881 Black White Flight: This cock (Boecxstaen strain) has sired six winners and is the grand-sire of 15 winners. One son has six firsts.

4. THE PIGEON

If your desire is to be a successful pigeon-flyer, you should purchase birds of the highest quality. An honest pigeon fancier will never knowingly sell an inferior pigeon to a novice. Moreover, most successful pigeon-flyers have a soft spot for a beginner. They will almost always sell you birds out of their very best stock and will take as much pride in your winning as if they themselves had won the race. This is especially true if you attend meetings of your local Racing Pigeon Club and let everyone know that you are in the market for good birds.

Obtaining Birds

Do not take pigeons from everyone who offers, but pick one or two top flyers and purchase birds from the family that has brought each champion flyer the most success. If you take birds from everyone who offers, you may win a few races but you will never become a champion and eventually will fail completely. The reason for this is that if you acquire many different families of pigeons it is impossible to form any type of breeding plan (and an intelligent breeding plan should be part of your racing strategy). The first birds you purchase should be your future breeding stock.

Do not purchase a team of youngsters and start flying. It is best to keep pigeons for at least six months before you plan on flying young birds. This allows you time to learn how to take care

A terrific breeding cock, Belge 62 6393765 Blue Bar is the sire of four winners (one daughter has over 20 diplomas) and the grand-sire of eight winners. The band had to be cut off this bird because his leg grew so big.

of them. Too often novices are so anxious to fly their pigeons that they rush into it before they know how to handle their birds. The result of such anxiousness is always discouragement and, if the pattern continues, complete failure. Be patient and you will most likely be a success.

Birds may also be purchased through the national pigeon magazines. When buying, do not buy from anybody but the known champions.

The Pedigree

When purchasing birds always ask for pedigrees and complete race and breeding records. A good pigeon-flyer always keeps accurate records.

A pedigree is the breeding record of each individual bird and should include all the important information pertaining to racing, distance flown, color, and special markings of the outstanding flyers. Accurate pedigrees help in many different ways. A good family of pigeons has characteristics that are unmistakable. For instance, a local fancier has an outstanding pair of breeders, but only the male offspring make good flyers while the hens are always lost. Nevertheless, the hens of this pair also make good breeders. In some families, certain-colored birds will make better breeders than flyers.

It would seem that to purchase winners and breed them together, you would have immediate success. Due to the

Himself a winner of two firsts and other diplomas, IF 67 HPC 1638 Dark Check (a Havenith-Huysken Van Riel cross cock) has sired two winners. This bird is a widowhood cock.

heterozygous nature of the racing pigeon [it possesses two gametes for each characteristic], definite breeding rules are impossible. This is why it is advisable to get related birds and breed according to pedigrees and race results. You will learn more from pedigrees, breeding records, and personal note-keeping than from any other source. Do not rely on your memory.

An advantage of buying from a top flyer is that you are sure of receiving birds in perfect health. This alone is worth the money paid for the pigeons. Another advantage is that an established family of birds already has the physical characteristics desired, thus saving you years of selection and breeding. (See Chapter 19 on showing for physical qualities.)

Knowing Your Pigeons

As described in Chapter 1, pigeons have always been a part of Man's life. It is hard to say why they were chosen. The reason could very well be that the pigeon has character. It will take years of personal observation to understand this statement.

Spend as much time as possible with the birds. Talk to them, move about slowly and treat them gently. Once they have confidence in you, they will know that no harm will ever come to them. Once a bird has been handled roughly, he will never forget and his fear of you will be sensed by the entire loft. The pigeon loves his home, whether it is a mansion or just a few orange crates. This is where he was born. His love for home is as great as any other living creature's. With this knowledge, and knowing how to handle the birds, you eventually will be crowned a champion.

When observing your pigeons, take special notes on each one's personality: Is he or she calm or wild? Active or lazy? Does he fight for his perch or is he easily driven off? Does he learn quickly? (This is most important. There has never been a champion that was slow to learn.) These are just a few things to look for. The physical qualities of each pigeon should also be observed. Observe which birds get fat the easiest and which ones stay lean. Also find out what birds are stronger on the wing and

Another widowhood cock and Havenith-Huysken Van Riel Cross, SC 66 HPC 925 Dark Check has 11 flights in each wing. "The Eleven Flighter" won 17 diplomas up to 340 miles until he broke a wing. He is the sire of four winners and grand-sire of three. "The Eleven Flighter" has yellow eyes.

never seem to tire. If a bird becomes sick, take notes about the nature of the illness and its recurrences. Notes of this nature may seem foolish, but the fact is you want to breed for good qualities, and if you eliminate birds through personal observation, it will save you years of hit-and-miss breeding. Almost every champion pigeon that has ever flown has had superior qualities, both physical and mental. It is rare when a champion has one and not the other.

When bringing the birds home for the first time, separate them by sexes. Now you are ready to feed and water them.

5. FEEDING

There has probably been more written on feeding than on any other subject related to pigeons. This has always been the most controversial subject. This chapter will give you a general knowledge of what and how to feed. The importance of choosing the right food and feeding in the right way cannot be over-emphasized. The fancier who learns to feed correctly will win his share of races. Food gives the elements for proper growth and fuel to nourish the body and produce heat and energy.

What to Feed

Every pigeon fancier should understand the scientific and chemical values of pigeon feed. The food requirements of pigeons come in two main forms: carbohydrates and proteins. Carbohydrates are a compound of carbon with hydrogen and oxygen, such as sugar, starch, and cellulose. Protein is one of a class of nitrogenous compounds, such as albumin, fibrin, and casein, which forms animal tissues. The gelatinous semi-transparent substance obtained from albumin, fibrin or casein is the essential nutritive element of food.

To start with, purchase the best-grade feed on the market. There are a number of top-quality commercial feed-mixtures available. After a little experience, you may add different types of grains to increase the quality of the mixture. Make a habit of buying the best: do not settle for a lesser quality for the sake of

Hand-feeding your birds is one of the best ways to get to know them and also to keep a careful check on their health.

a few dollars. Many fanciers have ruined years of breeding and flying just by using a poor quality of feed. If you find the feed bill is too high, do not sacrifice quality, but cut down on the amount of pigeons you keep. Following is a chart of the most important grains to feed and a break-down of their constituents.

Table I. Grains and Their Constituent Nutrients

Top Quality Grains	Dry Matter %	Digestible Protein %	Digestible Carbohydrates %	Digestible Oil %	Fibre %	Total Digestible Nutrients %
Maize (corn)	87.2	7.1	65.7	3.9	2.2	83.7
Wheat	89.8	11.3	64.0	1.2	1.6	89.8
Rice (brown)	88.6	6.3	75.8	0.2	0.4	69.1
Kafir	88.9	7.7	60.5	3.0	1.9	80.1
Barley	90.4	9.3	62.2	1.2	4.5	90.4
Buckwheat	85.9	8.5	42.3	1.9	14.4	64.4
Oats	86.7	8.0	62.2	1.2	4.5	91.7
Maple peas	86.0	19.4	49.9	1.0	5.4	90.5
Tic beans	85.7	20.1	44.1	1.2	7.1	*
Vetches	86.7	22.9	45.8	1.5	6.0	*
Peanuts	94.7	27.1	*	*	2.5	139.9
Linseed	93.6	21.4	18.3	34.7	5.5	108.7
Sunflower	93.4	14.6	10.3	30.7	28.1	87.8
Hemp	91.1	13.7	16.8	29.3	15.0	*
Dried yeast	92.0	35.6	29.2	0.2	0.5	74.6
Soybeans	90.2	32.8	*	*	4.5	86.2

*Indicates percentage not known

This chart gives you a general idea of the nutritive values of the most-used grains in commercial mixes. It will take years of experimenting to find the right feed-mixture. Many fanciers use different mixes for different times of the year: There is the breeding mixture (high in protein), the short-race mixture, the long-distance mixture, and the winter mixture. Some fanciers even feed their young birds differently. As you can see, there is much to learn. Do not feel that just by reading, you will be a success. It takes years of experimenting to find the correct system for you.

The quality of the grain has proved to be just as important as the varieties given. The major requirement for all mixtures is that every grain must be thoroughly seasoned. No matter how high the quality of the grains you use or how clean the feed is, if the grains have not been thoroughly dried and seasoned, the feed will always cause problems. When unseasoned grains are given, the pigeons' digestive systems become upset, dysentery sets in, the droppings become watery, weight is rapidly lost, and within days the birds most likely will die. The best way to check grains is to pinch and bite them. A good, sound grain will be hard and will break into hard, brittle pieces.

When grains become wet, there are forms of mould which will attack it. Because many moulds are invisible to the naked eye, it is sometimes impossible to detect bad grains, and many illnesses can arise from feeding such mouldy feed. Any feed that is doubtful should be disposed of. Sprouting grains should never be fed, since any grain that has germinated and shows a sprout is poison to pigeons.

All feed should be free of dust and foreign matter. The amount of dirt found in mixtures almost always is a good indicator of the quality of the mixture. Never feed any mixture that contains weevils, or any that has been contaminated by mice or rats. You may say to yourself that you will take a chance on feeding because the feed cost so much. But why run the risk of losing many birds to an epidemic? You can eliminate the risk of contamination if you store the grain correctly.

Storage

Correct storage of feed is another issue that cannot be ignored. Feed should be kept in a dry, cool, clean, rodent-free area. Feed, next to water, is the highest source of contamination, so take considerable precautions in storing it. Good, sound feedbins should be constructed. *Do not make them solid*, but have the fronts covered with heavy wire and fine screening, so that air can circulate through the feed. Air is very important in keeping the grains from spoiling. Build the bins so that they are easy to clean and are rodent-proof. If you purchase more feed than will fit into the bins, it will not hurt the grain to be left in the original unopened bags. If you have purchased small seeds like linseed

Feedbins like this one, having a wired or screened front, permit air circulation and thus guard your pigeons' feed from mould and other contaminations.

and hemp seed, store them in air-tight gallon jars. All feed and grit should be stored so that they are completely free from any forms of contamination.

Feeders

Every fancier has his own means in which to feed his birds. Many "patent"-type feeders and hoppers are available at the feed stores or through the pigeon magazines' order forms. You can also build a feeder of your own design. The reason for the feeder

Covered feeders that protect the feed from pigeon droppings are a must. Never feed your birds from an open bowl or tray.

The same feeder with the top removed for refilling. Here a fancier is scooping grit in.

is to keep the feed clean and free from the birds' droppings. Some fanciers place the feed on an open tray or even on the loft floor, but why run the risk of contamination when hopper-feeders are clean and easy to use? You should also keep the grit in containers so it cannot be soiled by droppings.

Grit

A properly constituted mineral mixture is another requirement to successful pigeon-flying. This mineral mixture is called GRIT. It is only through grit that your pigeons can obtain their vital

Close-up of a flyer's daily ration of grit. Be sure that you give your pigeon fresh grit every day.

minerals. The mineral requirement for pigeons is very high, and this can be seen by the large amounts of grit eaten. This is why *fresh grit should be given daily*. Without grit it would be impossible for pigeons to digest their food. Grit is stored in the gizzard, which is a vital organ to the pigeon. It is here that the grain is ground, with the aid of grit, into pieces small enough to be completely digested. Buy grit of the highest quality.

A proper grit mixture helps to keep your birds in good health. It also promotes rapid growth in youngsters and almost entirely eliminates soft-shelled eggs. The U.S. Department of Agriculture has recommended the following grit mixture:

40% medium-sized crushed oyster shell
35% limestone or granite grit
10% medium-sized hardwood charcoal
5% ground bone
5% ground limestone
4% salt
1% Venetian red

How to Feed

To eliminate confusion, the whole story of feeding will not be fully discussed in this chapter. There are various seasons to the pigeon's year: the breeding season, the short-distance, long-distance, and young-bird racing seasons, and the moult. Each season requires a different method of feeding, and these methods will be discussed in their proper chapters.

The last young-bird race is usually flown in early October, and from this time on the birds must be fed with the idea of having them in breeding condition. They must be fed twice a day. It does not hurt to feed them heavy, but make sure that they do not get overly fat. Fat is just as unhealthful to pigeons as it is to any other form of life. Do not let feed lie in front of the birds at all times. This leads to lazy eating habits and obesity.

Water

Water is the single most important thing on this earth, for without it nothing would live. A pigeon may go days without feed and never show any ill effects, but 24 hours without water may damage a bird so badly that he can never recover. Change the birds' water at least twice a day. It should never be allowed to get dirty, for water is Number One as a means of spreading disease. The waterers should be above floor level and placed so that it is impossible for them to be fouled by dirt and droppings. *The waterer should be washed every time the water is changed*, and at least twice a month you should clean it thoroughly with boiling water. This eliminates algae and bacteria that colonize in the container. You can purchase waterers at a feed store or through the pigeon magazines. Whatever system you use, make sure it keeps the water *clean*.

To show the importance of water in maintaining healthy racing pigeons, a Pittsburgh fancier related the following account of what happened a few years ago:

For two weeks, business kept him from spending any time with his pigeons. In fact, the birds were fed and watered only once a day. At this single feeding they received feed equivalent to two "ordinary" feedings, but the following day there was always feed left from the previous day. Each day, even though the temperature was about 32° F. (0° C.), the birds' appetites never seemed to increase. The owner did not realize what was happening until he went to the loft to pick birds for the annual Show. Out of 44 pigeons, not one had any body form. Each one felt, to the touch, as if it had just come off a hard race. There was enough feed left in the hopper, so what was the matter? Well, it was simple: with the low temperatures, it did not take the water long to freeze solid. So actually the birds were getting only one good drink a day. And for a pigeon, that is not enough. The birds were dehydrating from lack of water. Even in cold weather a pigeon still demands a lot of water to keep in top health.

Needless to say, this Pittsburgh fancier was completely eliminated from show-competition and he lost an entire year. If this situation had gone on any longer, he may have ruined his entire loft of birds. In reading about this fancier's neglect, you should realize the importance of proper feeding habits. Start off right: by forming good feeding habits. And *never change them*.

6. THE BREEDING SEASON

There are three breeding plans available to the fancier: outcrossing, inbreeding, and linebreeding. Outcrossing means the mating of unrelated birds. Inbreeding is the mating of only related pigeons and linebreeding means that the birds are bred to the male line with only an occasional outcross. As with the human race, it is only the male that can carry on the line. Only the male child can continue the family name, and the same is true with the pigeon line.

You must breed to the male line because of the influence of the sex gene. It is a known fact that both the cock and the hen pass their sex genes to their sons, but only the cock can pass his sex gene to his daughters. (The hen is unable to do this.) Because of this factor, if you breed to a female line the cocks become henny-looking, are undersized, and not as robust. Fanciers who have tried to build their loft through the hen line have all failed.

You should give plenty of time to figuring out the best way to mate your birds. If this is your first year of breeding, ask the fancier whom you purchased your birds from to help you.

Mating the Birds

If you already have a family of birds that are closely related and fly well, then breed to keep this family intact. Always remember when breeding: if you own a successful family of

Introduce a nest bowl into the nest box on the second day after mating. Once the cock has driven the hen to nest, the couple will settle down, as the pigeons have here. The first egg is usually laid 10 days after the mating.

pigeons, keep this family together; do not, through careless breeding habits, let this family deteriorate.

Some fanciers mate their birds on paper, through the use of pedigrees, and some mate strictly by past race and breeding

Stock-birds are a vital factor in every loft. Here, AU 66 NWC 1713 Blue Check. This Huysken Van Riel Cock has never been flown, but has sired eight winners and is the grand-sire of seven winners. A pearl-eye, this stock bird is, himself, the son of the famous No. 228 Huysken Van Riel.

A hen should give an impression of daintiness in contrast to a cock. This Havenith hen, Belge 60 6657018 Blue Check (a chestnut-eye), proved to be a remarkable breeder: she is the dam of five winners, the grand dam of 11 winners and great-grand dam of 20 winners.

results. Finally, some just open the doors and let the birds choose their own mates. The last is the lazy-man's way. Whatever way you choose, it is essential to keep the breeding-quality high and breed nothing but extra-healthy pigeons. If you do not own a proven pair of breeders, the first years of breeding will be guess-work. It takes 3 to 4 years to establish a loft: be patient and you will eventually become a winner.

Sexing

In most cases the cock is larger than the hen. Also, the cock has a larger, dominant head—one giving the appearance that the eyes are set higher in the head. The beak, wattles, and eye cere are usually heavier in males, and the neck is much thicker. A good male should have an over-all appearance of masculinity, while the hen should be small and dainty. The male is generally aggressive, almost always starting fights.

NOTE: If you have a mating that did not work the year before and you want to split up the pair, a good point to remember is that the hen must be taken to the cock and not vice versa. The nest box always belongs to the cock, not the hen. Even though the cock will take a new nest box, he will still go back to his old nest box and fight to retain both of them. So remember in mating your birds: always give the cock his old nest, thus eliminating unnecessary fighting.

Pairing Up

In the temperate zones, the breeding season usually starts late in winter, and it is best to choose a time when you can spend a couple of days with the birds. One week before mating, let the males choose their nest boxes, and when every male is settled to his nest, it is time for mating. The hens should be locked into the nests with their future mates.

Almost instantly courtship begins: with a proud masculine strut, the cock parades up and down in front of his hen, cooing, strutting, spreading his tail, bobbing his head and spinning about. Very often the hen will show her excitement by spreading her tail and then strutting up to the male and giving him a gentle nudge. Some males may get overly aggressive and harm the hen. If you see this over-aggression coming on, separate the pair. It often helps to put them in a partition by themselves until they have mated.

The hen rarely resists the cock's advances, but will show acceptance by a softer cooing and strutting about, and the courtship is completed with a kiss, or billing. The male opens his beak, and the female puts her beak in his mouth. He then gently closes his beak and pushes down on her beak, giving the impression that they are playing tug-of-war. The hen will run her beak through the coverlets on the back of his head and neck. Soon after the courtship, copulation usually occurs. The hen crouches down and separates her wings very slightly. The cock mounts her back, and as the hen turns her tail to one side, the sexual act is completed.

A pigeon will lay her eggs in an empty nest bowl, but you should never permit this to happen. Here, a hen has already laid her first egg in a properly insulated nest bowl. The egg will not be incubated until the second egg of this round is laid.

Introduce a nest bowl into the nest on the second day. On the fifth day, the male begins to drive the hen to nest. His temperament changes from a loving mate to being overly aggressive, and he will chase the hen about the loft, pecking at her head and very often slapping her with one of his wings. He will not let her eat or drink, but do not worry because no harm comes to her. His driving will stop when she enters the nest.

Nesting Material

The nest bowl may be of many different types. Pottery nest bowls, disposable papier-mâché, wooden salad bowls, and even breadbaskets have been used. An ideal nest bowl is one made out of wood. It has an 8″ square bottom and should be 4″ deep. Being wood, it should be painted once a year with a fine grade of creosote.

A pigeon will lay its eggs in an empty bowl, but this is not advisable. The gathering of nesting material is an important part of the sexual process and it is another way that the male shows his acceptance of the nest.

The following materials have been successfully used by pigeon breeders because they are available locally and are cheaper or easier to obtain than anything else: twigs, sawdust, hay, straw, tobacco stems, pine needles, and Stay-Dri. Every one of these is good and has something to recommend it. Stay-Dri (a commercial preparation of shredded sugar-cane stocks) seems to be best, as it is very absorbent and easy for the birds to work with in making their nests. Because of its small texture, the nest has a tendency to pack better and stay warmer. Also, there is less chance that the eggs will roll about.

Laying and Incubation

Pigeons follow a regular breeding cycle, which starts with the mating. Five days later, the male starts driving the female to nest, and the hen usually lays her first egg on the tenth day after mating has occurred. The laying of the eggs is timed, with the first egg being laid in early evening between 5 and 7 o'clock. The second egg is laid in mid-morning, approximately 45 hours later. Very little attention is paid to the first egg, but do not worry. It is Nature's way of having both eggs hatch at the same time.

The eggs take 18 days to hatch, or roughly four weeks from the time of mating. Approximately 16 days after these first eggs hatch, the hen will lay the first egg of the second round. Remember that this time-cycle may vary with different pairs.

Do not handle the hen when she is close to laying: it is too easy to cause internal damage. To understand why, you must know something of the process of egg laying: The process of egg formation begins only when the hen receives enough stimulation to start her reproductive system functioning. The male's sperm, upon copulation, enters the hen's oviduct in great numbers and the spermatozoa work their way up the duct into the hen's infundibulum and into the thin, albuminous, glairy (eggy) liquid. Here they are stored and retain their fertilizing ability for approximately 14 days. Fertilization may occur before the egg leaves its capsule or as soon as the germinal disc is exposed. It may also occur at any time from the egg's separation from the ovary until the eggshell is acquired.

Two of the hen's follicles start to grow in size, gradually filling with yolk. Growth continues until the yolk of the first egg reaches its full development. The egg yolk is first formed in the ovary, and for $4\frac{1}{2}$ days its growth is rapid. A small speck on the side of the yolk is the beginning of the embryo. On the night of the fourth day, the yolk leaves the ovary and begins its way to the oviduct. The movement of the yolk occurs at night because there is no movement of the hen to endanger her safety. If the hen is disturbed at this time, the yolk may fall into the body cavity, and this will cause serious trouble. It is during the yolk's passage through the oviduct that it receives the albumen. The albumen (white of the egg) is the food that the embryo receives to exist upon until hatching. At the lower end of the oviduct the yolk and the albumen receive glandular secretions that form the layers of parchmentlike shell membrane. Passing onward, it reaches the uterus, where it receives its shell. At this time the egg may be felt between the vent bones. The egg stays in the lower portion of the oviduct for approximately 45 hours. Any length of time over this may smother the germ, which will cause the embryo to die. So as you can see, much can go wrong if you handle a hen that is about to lay. Therefore it is best to just let the pigeons alone. Frequent disturbances can only do harm.

Incubation of the eggs does not begin until the second egg is laid. Then the cock and hen both incubate the eggs. The hen sits at night until mid-morning, when the male takes over. About mid-afternoon, the hen returns to relieve the male. There may be variations to this, with either the cock or hen sitting longer than normal or even showing little desire to share incubation. Chilling should not take place in the later development of the egg, for

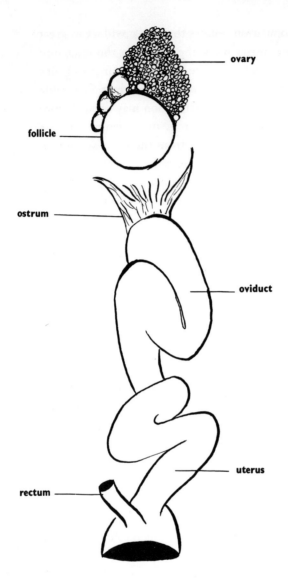

ovary

follicle

ostrum

oviduct

uterus

rectum

Diagram of the reproductive system of a hen. Never handle a hen when she is close to laying; it is all too easy to injure her.

this almost always leads to death of the embryo. For this reason, great care should be taken not to disturb brooding pigeons. *Leave them alone.*

Eggs should never be allowed to become soiled by droppings. When the droppings dry they prevent air from reaching the embryo through the porous shell. If an egg becomes soiled, wet it with lukewarm water and very gently wipe it clean.

Check the inside of the shell as soon as a squab has hatched: excess blood or a dark film means you will have a weak youngster on your hands.

Proper records are essential: the correct dates of laying and hatching must be recorded. Special notes should be taken on each individual pair, such as did they mate easily or was there much hesitation or fighting? Was the hen overly slow in laying? Or was it the male's fault? These plus many other observations should be taken.

A Word about Hens

One of the hardest things for a beginner to find is good breeding hens. The ratio of good breeding cocks as compared with good breeding hens may be as high as 10 to 1. The authors' personal opinion is that from the time the hen hatches she is at an unfair disadvantage. Since the cock is more robust, he always seems to get the lion's share at mealtime. Also, the young hens cannot take as much punishment in training and races. Most fanciers treat the cock and hen as equals. If they had a little sympathy towards the hen they would find out that it would reward them threefold in the long run. One good example of this is Ed Topoleski of the Pittsburgh area. Ed always babies his hens and by the number of good breeding and flying hens in his loft you can come to only one conclusion:

that it pays to have patience and to spare the hens any undue hardships. The authors have never found a successful loft where there was not an abundance of good hens. You may have the world's most valuable breeding cock, but without a hen of almost equal value he is useless.

Raising Healthy Youngsters

Healthy youngsters can be raised only if the parents are in top physical condition. If either of the parents is weak in any way, the egg will not be 100 per cent right. Thus inferior youngsters will develop. Only a healthy egg will give you healthy youngsters.

It takes 48 hours for the squab to hatch out. So on the sixteenth day, check for signs of chipping, or pipping. With its egg-tooth the embryonic squab begins chipping at the larger end of the egg and works at this until a complete circle has been made. The squab then forces its way out by shoving with its feet until its head and shoulders break the shell into two sections. After hatching, check the inside of the shell to make sure it is relatively clean. If the shell contains a dark covering and an excess of blood, you know the youngster is weak. Never help a squab to hatch from its egg: a healthy squab never needs help.

During incubation, the cock and the hen both form pigeon milk in their crops. As soon as the eggs hatch either parent is able to feed this milk by placing the squab's beak inside its own mouth and, by regurgitation, pumping the pigeon milk into the squab's crop.

Pigeon milk is formed in the parent's crop by the hormone prolactin, just as mammals' milk is formed. The composition of this milk is high in water and protein, low in fats, and almost void of carbohydrates. It is the squab's only diet until the fourth day when small grains are added to the milk. The amount of pigeon milk decreases daily until about the tenth day when only solid grains are fed.

Feeding correctly at this time is most important. Unlike the case with chickens, the laying of eggs, incubation, and raising of the young is a very strenuous task for a pigeon. It would not hurt

A pigeon should not be disturbed like this when brooding. If you upset the parent(s) enough, they will leave the eggs to chill and die. Insect pests and rodents are another cause of deserted nests.

to increase the feedings to three times a day, and the amount fed is most important. After the parents eat their fill, they pump the contents of their crops into the youngsters. After the parents have eaten enough to feed the youngsters, there should still be enough grain left in the hopper for the parents to receive their own nourishment. Too often a fancier neglects his feeding habits and the breeders become run down.

If the breeders get too badly out of condition, the second and third round of youngsters will not be as healthy and robust as the first, and you may do permanent damage to the adult breeders.

Do not forget to add fresh grit daily and always check the waterers. The intake of water during breeding season almost triples.

Feeding Greens

Much can be said pro and con feeding greens. Those fanciers against feeding greens feel that it makes the droppings too watery and that there is a high risk that worms will enter the pigeon's body through tiny worm-eggs attached to the leaves. Let us take each problem one at a time.

Watery droppings, caused by eating greens, never do the breeders any harm. If you feed your pigeons greens on Monday morning, by Tuesday evening the droppings should be back to normal. If wet droppings persist, some other factor is causing it and not the greens. Flyers should be fed greens only on Monday mornings, but *in lesser quantities*. Watch the droppings carefully, making sure they are round and firm by Tuesday. If you find the greens are too harsh on the flyers, then eliminate them during the Racing Season.

Continue feeding greens to the breeders and also to all birds during the winter. Racing condition and breeding condition are two different states of health in a pigeon. Always remember: What is good for one condition is not always good for the other.

The fanciers who are against feeding greens state that it might cause worms, but there has been no proof of this. The risk may be there, but the risk of pigeons getting worms from greens is no higher than their getting them from any other form of feeding. Thoroughly rinsing the greens first may reduce the risk. Worms have been found in both the pigeon that is fed greens and the pigeon that never gets them. Good advice to any fancier is never to draw any conclusions until you are sure of all the facts.

Greens do more good than can be imagined. Not only are they beneficial to the birds, but greens give them a more varied diet. Pigeons love all forms of greens, and the excitement they show when fed greens is sufficient reason to feed them. The best source of Vitamin A is in the bright green and dark yellow vegetables. Following is a list of greens that may be fed and how to prepare them:

1. Cabbage	Chop into pieces
2. Lettuce	Cut into small pieces or feed the whole leaf *(Do not feed lettuce to race birds.)*
3. Leaf spinach	Cut into small pieces or feed the whole leaf
4. Carrots	Chop into small pieces
5. Dandelions	Cut only the stems into small pieces, or the whole dandelion may be dug up and fed, roots and all
6. Water cress	Cut into small pieces or feed the whole leaf
7. Garlic	Cut into small pieces and place into the pigeon's mouth, making sure they are swallowed
8. Celery leaves	Feed whole
9. Alfalfa	Feed whole
10. Kale	Chop into pieces
11. Parsley	Feed whole
12. Turnip tops	Chop into pieces
13. Chicory	Feed whole

Iodized salt, red pepper, or garlic salt may be added to the greens. Do not add all three at once, but any one of them is ideal. If you feed the greens as directed, your birds will benefit most highly.

Food Supplements

Every fancier has his own ideas on supplementing the diet. Each supplement is good in its own right, and again, it is strictly one's own personal choice.

Pigeon pellets, along with the regular diet, are one of the best supplements available to feed breeding pigeons. Pellets are not recommended for flyers because they have the tendency to cause watery droppings. Following is a chart showing the many grains and by-products that are in most pellets now on the market.

Table II. Pellets and Their Constituents

Ingredient	Water %	Protein %	Carbohydrate %	Fibre %	Fat %
Alfalfa meal	7.8	20.0	41.1	18.0	2.5
Barley meal	11.0	11.5	66.5	6.0	2.0
Blood meal	9.7	80.0	3.8	1.0	1.0
Brewers' yeast	6.3	46.0	35.7	2.8	1.2
Buttermilk (dried)	7.6	32.4	43.3	none	5.0
Maize (corn) meal	15.0	8.9	68.9	2.0	3.9
Cottonseed meal	7.8	41.0	26.3	9.0	7.0
Fish meal	6.4	62.2	4.2	0.7	8.5
Kafir meal	7.1	11.0	71.1	2.5	2.5
Linseed meal	8.8	35.0	36.9	8.1	5.6
Meat scraps (dried)	6.2	60.0	1.1	2.4	8.8
Molasses	26.0	2.9	62.1	none	none
Oatmeal	9.3	15.0	64.4	2.0	7.4
Peanut meal	7.2	43.1	23.0	13.9	7.6
Rice	9.7	12.7	56.6	3.5	11.4
Rye meal	10.5	12.6	70.9	2.4	1.7
Milk (dried)	5.8	34.7	50.3	0.2	1.2
Soybean meal	9.4	46.1	31.8	5.9	1.0
Wheat-germ meal	7.1	26.0	none	2.5	8.0

As you can see, pellets are high in proteins, and proteins are very essential to rapid growth in squabs. Many pellets also include some form of medication to help combat disease. The breeders' feed-mixture should contain 80 per cent grain and 20 per cent pellets.

Cod liver oil is another very good supplement. Cod liver oil capsules may be given or the oil may be added directly to the grain. Both are available at health shops. Since the oil is messy to feed, it is best to add Vionate to the oil-covered grains. Vionate is a powder very high in vitamin and mineral content. It may be purchased at your local feed or pet shop. Add enough Vionate so that the grains are completely covered. It may also be added to the grit, or you can feed it by itself. Following is a list of supplements that are sometimes used by different fanciers:

1. Myzon — A powder added to the water; very high in vitamins and preventative medicines
2. Dried brewers' yeast — A powder added to the water; very high in protein
3. Lemon juice — Added to the water
4. Wheat-germ oil — Feed same way as cod liver oil
5. Halibut oil — Feed same way as cod liver oil

6. Honey	Add to hot water and let cool; restores energy
7. Herring meal	Very good source of Vitamin B-12
8. Egg shells	Crush and add to grit
9. Dirt	Earth dug from the ground; feed separately
10. Kilpatric's minerals	Feed separately; very high in mineral content
11. Wins more	Add to water; very high in vitamin and mineral content
12. Magnesium block	Feed separately

These are just a few of the many hundreds of different supplements you may add to your pigeons' diet. It is impossible to feed everything that you hear or read about. It is best to choose only a few and stick with them. Continually changing a pigeon's diet is very bad, for pigeons are a slave to habit, and any change can thoroughly disrupt a pigeon's entire system.

Banding the Birds

When the squeaker is between 7 and 10 days of age, it should be banded. It is not always necessary to handle the youngster. Turn it in its nest until the right leg is accessible. Take great care not to hurt or frighten it. Put the band on upside down and slip it over the first three toes. The fourth toe will bend backwards

The squeaker's first experience of its master is at the banding. Therefore, take great care not to hurt or frighten the youngster.

Always put the band on upside down, for easy reading. The band is to slip over the first three toes, while the fourth toe bends gently backwards against the leg.

against the leg as you slide the band over the foot. Very carefully, ease the fourth toe clear of the band. You put the band on upside down so that when the bird is being held correctly, the band will be easier to read. This saves time when the birds are being countermarked for the races.

When banding, make sure that the correct band number is marked in your breeding records. Keeping accurate breeding records is very important in building a winning loft.

Checking the Squeaker

It is very important to make sure that the squeaker is in good health. A healthy squeaker should have feed in its crop at all times and should lie quietly in the nest. A noisy youngster is in some sort of distress.

The squeaker's droppings should be round and firm, without an excess of water. There may be some water in the droppings, but not to the point of diarrhea.

When handled, the bird should be dead weight, have bright alert eyes, and feel strong. To make sure there is no obstruction, check the throat and navel for canker.

Any youngster that has had any severe set-back should be destroyed. Health that has been lost at an early age can never be restored.

Weaning

At four weeks of age the youngsters should be weaned. Place them in their own partition and at this time make doubly sure that you have recorded the correct band number and color under the correct parents. Once the youngsters are weaned, your memory may fail you, causing discrepancies in the breeding records.

Pigeons tending a nest of squabs often have to be fed three times a day. The parents' water intake, until the squabs are weaned, almost triples.

Racing-pigeon squeakers should be removed from the nest box at about four weeks of age and put in the young-bird section of your loft. This youngster is 23 days old and almost ready to wean. When the youngster at the left drops his first flight feather, this will mark the end of the weaning crisis.

For the first week or 10 days, these youngsters should be given the utmost attention for they do not know how to eat and drink and it is up to you to help them learn. They should be fed small quantities at least four times a day. Feed them only the smallest grains when they are first weaned. After they are eating well, you must teach them to eat larger grains. You do this by giving them the large grains such as corn and peas first at each feeding and not giving the smaller grains until the larger are eaten.

Another problem that arises is that some birds will eat only certain grains. You can correct this by feeding in small amounts and forcing them, through hunger, to eat everything before you give any more.

It is of the utmost importance that the youngsters find the water. If you see a youngster that is blinking and refuses to eat, most likely it has not found the water. Take it and place its head into the water. For the first few days, it would not hurt to place the newly weaned youngsters' heads into the water. If they are healthy and alert, it takes only a few days until they are eating and drinking.

Make a special effort to keep the water clean. Grit is essential at this time, and the youngsters should have access to plenty of fresh, clean grit. Frequent baths should also be given. Three a week is most beneficial for youngsters at this age. Immediately after bathing remove the water, since the youngsters have little discrimination between dirty and clean water and may drink the dirty bath water.

Keep the young-bird section as clean and dry as possible. Just after weaning, the squabs' resistance to disease may be down, so check again for canker in the throat and navel.

The dropping of the first flight feather marks the end of the weaning crisis and the growing of this flight shows that the acclimation of the youngsters is going well.

Second Rounds

Approximately 16 days after the youngsters have hatched, the hen will lay the first egg of the second round. You should place a second nest bowl into the nest 14 days after hatching of the first round, so the eggs are not laid in the same nest as the youngsters. In this way there is less chance that the new eggs will be broken or soiled.

The second round is just as important as the first, so take all the same precautions. You will find that the second round has a tendency to mature faster than the first. This enables them to catch up in the moult and in their physical and mental abilities. Very often, too, they make just as good young-bird flyers.

Do not let the second round out with the first hatch until they have been taught loft procedure and are able to flock. Very often the first round drags the second too far from the loft. This is how you lose many second-round youngsters.

Third-round hatches often make excellent breeding stock. Here, "Pet Hen" who bred two first-prize winners and one fourth-prize winner in race competitions, the first year she was mated.

Third Rounds

Sometimes a third hatch is raised, with the first egg being laid 16 days after the hatching of the second round. Very often after the third round, the first egg of the fourth round is laid as early as 12 days after hatching. If the weather has turned warm, the parents do not have to sit so long on the squab. This is what causes the laying cycle to start earlier.

If you raise a third round, it is advisable to keep them separate from the first and second. The reason is that the flock is tripping and these youngsters are close to being trained for the races.

Late hatches are too often lost and they also have an adverse effect on your flock by causing confusion by their dumbness. It is advisable to save a few pair of third hatches from your best breeders for future stock-birds.

If you raise a third team, you must train them exactly as you did the first and second hatches, only separately. When the hen lays her fourth round, replace the eggs with dummy eggs. (Dummy eggs are made of wood or glass and may be purchased through a pigeon-supply dealer.) After weaning the third round, it is time to separate the breeders so they can go through a good moult.

7. THE MOULT

To better understand the moult, one must first know the different types of feathers. Each kind of feather is for a different purpose and each kind is moulted differently.

Feathers serve as an outer coat that overlaps in such a way that the pigeon's body heat (75° F.; 41.7° C.) is held in, thus keeping the bird warm. The feather begins within the external skin and grows outwards. The FOLLICLE (feather pit) forms within the skin, and the feather grows outwards from the papilla which is at the base of the follicle. All feathers are high in protein content, and this is one reason why a pigeon needs a relatively high protein diet.

Down Feathers

Down feathers, known as PLUMULAE, are the yellow furlike covering that is found on all newly hatched squabs. As the youngster grows older, the down feathers fall off and are completely gone by the time the squabs are 4 weeks old.

Many fanciers believe that the more down feathers a squab has, the more robust and healthy he will be at maturity. Although this may be only theory, it would be interesting to mark in the breeding records whether the youngster was downless, short downed, or long downed. The only way to prove or disprove a theory is to keep records, weigh the facts, and arrive at an answer. When questions arise that you do not understand, it is always best to try and figure them out for yourself. This is especially true in pigeon-keeping because each loft is different and what is good for one flock may be bad for another.

Hair Feathers

Hair feathers (FILOPLUMES) are the hairlike feathers that lie under the contour feathers. They may be easily observed when the pigeon has been plucked.

Fluff Feathers

Fluff feathers (SEMIPLUMES) grow on the body and are found on the sides, undersides, vent area, rump area, and the underside of the tail. The fluffiness is caused by the small shaft and connecting barbules. A pigeon in good health should moult these feathers the year round. When a pigeon is being caught, these feathers are often pulled out and are the least likely to show fret marks.

Very often in the rump and vent area the larger fluff feathers fail to come out of the shaft, and this failure causes large pinfeathers to form. This condition has been proven to be a diet deficiency, and you should take the proper steps to correct it.

Contour Feathers

Contour feathers (PLUMAE) are the body feathers that overlap to form the pigeon's protective coat. They are most important for keeping in the pigeon's body heat, keeping the elements off the pigeon, and forming a smooth surface so that air may move over the pigeon's body and help it in flight.

The large flight feathers that enable the pigeon to fly and the tail feathers (RETRICES) that are used as the rudder and part of the braking system are the largest of the contour feathers. The flight feathers and the tail, although different in shape, are similar in structure. Down the middle of each feather runs a hollow tube called the QUILL. The quill fits into a socket and is held by internal muscles. The barbs grow out of both sides of the quill, and there are as many as 1,200 barbs on each feather. From each barb come tiny barbules, and on each barbule there are two

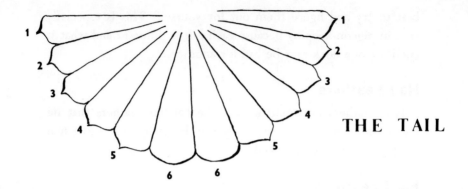

THE TAIL

The 12 retrices act as the pigeon's rudder and a part of the bird's braking system.

kinds of barbicels: the hooked and the non-hooked. These barbules and barbicels can be seen clearly only with the aid of a microscope.

The barbicels are arranged in such a way that when the feather is being pressed on the downward motion of the wing, they automatically lock into each other and thus form an air-tight surface that gives the pigeon lift. On the upward stroke the barbicels automatically unhook and allow the barbules to separate and the air to pass through.

There are portions of a pigeon's body where feathers do not grow. All contour feathers grow in FEATHER TRACTS (patterns from which the feathers grow). These tracts can be seen on youngsters ten days old. When you look at or handle a pigeon you get the impression that the feathers grow out of the entire body. This is not so: they grow out of only the feather tracts, and as the feather blooms into a full feather, they overlap to form a solid covering.

Starting the Moult

The moult is the natural process in which the pigeon renews all of its feathers (excluding the secondaries) once a year. The

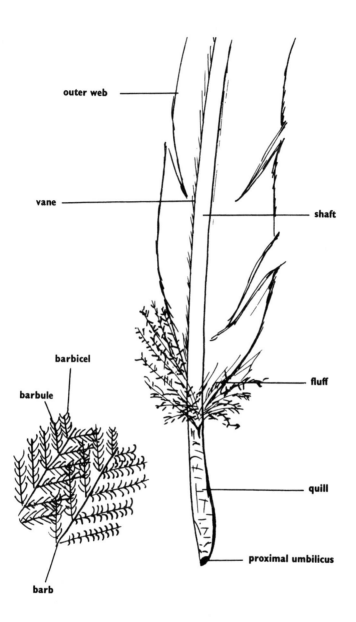

outer web

vane

barbicel

barbule

barb

shaft

fluff

quill

proximal umbilicus

CONTOUR FEATHER

The interlocking of the barbicels gives the pigeon lift. Then, when
the barbicels unhook, the barbules separate and the wing is no longer
an air-tight surface.

moult is continuous from the daily moulting of the fluff feathers until the heavy moult that occurs in the fall of the year.

In young birds the moult begins shortly after weaning when the Number One primary is dropped. Soon after the dropping of the second flight, the moult of the small body feathers and the wing coverts begins. A small percentage of neck and head feathers are also moulted, but it is not until later that the heavy moult begins.

The feather can be described as dying at the socket so that whenever the bird flies, the movement loosens the feather from the dried-out socket until it falls. When observing a flight feather that has been dropped you will notice that the base of the quill and the very tip (INFERIOR UMBILICUS) are completely dried out. A flight that has not been dropped has body fluid within the quill, which has entered through the inferior umbilicus opening.

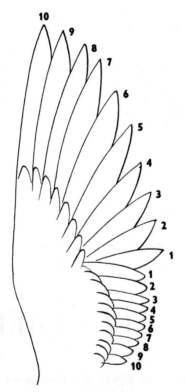

Moulting of the secondary flights usually does not begin until a bird has dropped its fifth primary.

THE WING

Within hours of the feather's dropping, a sheath containing the new feather will begin to grow from the socket. The sheath is actually a protective covering that holds in the valuable body fluids and blood so that the feather may grow without damage. The sheath is pushed outwards until the end of the feather protrudes from it. The feather will continue growing, with the sheath still protecting the lower portion, until it has taken the place of the old feather. If the feather, especially a flight feather, grows longer or thinner than normal, then you know that some type of deficiency is present. A pigeon that does not go through a good moult is not in a good state of health, and corrective measures must be taken.

Adult pigeons usually begin their moult with the laying of the second round. The primary flights are moulted in an order starting from one to ten; and upon moulting the fifth flight, the old bird begins to drop its coverts and proceeds into a heavy moult. The secondaries are not dropped in any particular order— in fact the birds do not always moult all of the secondaries.

As with the primaries, the tail feathers are moulted in a definite order. While moulting of the wing and tail feathers are going on, the small head, neck, and body feathers continue their moulting course: it takes at least six months to moult the entire body of feathers.

Ensuring a Good Moult

After the third round of youngsters are weaned, it is best to separate the breeders and flyers by sex. This takes away the strain of the breeding process and allows 100 per cent of the birds' strength for the moulting process. It has been proven time and again that a bird that does not go through a good moult does not perform well the following year. Pigeons that are allowed to continue to lay and raise youngsters hold back considerably on their moult and sometimes do not even complete it. For this reason pigeons should not be bred hard or late into the season.

During the moult many fanciers keep their pigeons indoors. This is a big mistake because the birds' muscles get flabby and the restriction upsets their digestive and respiratory systems.

A perfect wing.

Moulting pigeons should receive a fair amount of exercise. Make sure, though, that it is not extensive.

Regular baths are a must during the heavy moult: give the birds two baths a week. The larger the bath-pan the better: too small a pan creates fighting, and many of the shyer birds will go without a bath. A pan 4″ deep is ideal. A large, deep pan allows the birds space to lie about in the water and completely enjoy their bath.

Increase the protein content of your birds' diet during the moult. Also increase the grains of high oil content, especially linseed, rape, hemp, and canary seed. If you take proper care, there is not much to worry about in seeing your birds through a proper moult. Other than a slight change in diet and an extra bath there is really not much more that can be done.

This wing shows many fret marks and deformed flights. This hen is going through a bad moult and probably was not given the proper diet throughout the year, or may have been lost for a while.

Oil Gland or Preening Gland

The oil gland (UROPYGIAL) is found at the lower end of the rump right at the base of the tail feathers. The actual function of the oil or preening gland has not yet been ascertained. Following are a few well-founded theories on its use.

The oil contains fatty acids combined with octadecyl alcohol and ergosterol. Ergosterol when exposed to sunlight is converted into Vitamin D. One theory has it that the pigeon squeezes the oil gland to receive Vitamin D. [This may be only part of the function of the gland.]

The most-accepted theory is that, when preening, the pigeon receives oil from the gland simply by smearing the oil on its beak. With oil smeared on its beak the pigeon then commences to spread oil on its feathers as it preens. This oil-spreading protects the pigeon from water much in the way it does waterfowl.

During the process of courtship and mating the smell of the oil becomes much stronger, which leads some pigeon experts to believe that the preening gland acts in the same way as the sebaceous glands of mammals. The sebaceous gland gives off a distinct aroma that enables a mammal's mate to find it.

It has been observed that waterfowl preen more than any other class of birds. It has been proven that the more the birds preen, the more oil is found on their feathers. Scientists believe that the amount of preening has much to do with the amount of oil found on the feathers—oil that is their only protection against forms of precipitation.

Although this is only another theory, why could not the oil gland serve more than one purpose? It may very well be that the bird receives the oil on the feathers through preening, receives Vitamin D from this gland, and maybe utilizes the smell in being found by his (or her) mate. As you can see, there is still much to learn about the pigeon. Even the scientists have been unable to completely explain such phenomena as the homing instinct and the simple oil gland. Through your own experience maybe *you* will be the one to discover the facts on these subjects.

8. COLORS

Identifying colors on all breeds of pigeons is a very difficult thing to understand. The reason is that the different colors and patterns are so numerous, so varied, and so often blended together to form different patterns that it is next to impossible to know them. In one fancy variety alone, the Modena, there are 152 different color varieties. If one were to take into consideration every breed and variety, the color combinations would run into the thousands.

Another great difficulty in the matter of identifying colors is the fancier himself. It is amazing how many experienced fanciers are still confused on the correct color identification! After years of flying they cannot tell the difference between a blue-check, a dark-check, or a black checker—and many men still consider the silver, the dun, and the mealy as the same color variety when actually all three are different.

The Racing Pigeon's Colors

The principal color of the racing pigeon is blue: from the blue come all the blue-bars (stripes) and checkers (darker-shaded small feathers). The next most common color is red: from red come the red-checks, silvers and all related color varieties. Black is the third—and most uncommon—color variety of the racing pigeon.

This hen is a blue bar. SC 66 HPC 361 or "The Birthday Hen" is of the Havenith strain and has yellow eyes. Among her descendants are at least two long-distance winners and six winners at shorter distance.

Blue

Blue is not only the most common color variety; it is moreover the main color in the *Columba Livia* (the Wild Blue Rock Pigeon), which is said to be the origin of all domestic pigeons. In the Wild Blue Rock Pigeon, the body and wings are a blue and across the wings are two dark stripes or bars. The head and neck are usually slightly darker, with the tail being the same shade as the flights.

The blue in pigeons is not the deep or bright shades of blue which are found in other birds. It is closer to a light grey or a blue-grey, with many different shades running from very light blue to almost a dark grey or smoky-blue. This is probably where the most confusion arises when identifying the colors: many fanciers are unable to distinguish correctly among the different shades.

You may ask yourself what is so important about being correct in identifying the colors. The fact is that without proper color-identification, a true breeding strategy is almost impossible. As explained previously, certain colors in a particular family fly best while other-colored birds make better breeders. And to maintain correct records you must note the correct colors. If the pigeon is a checker, you must record whether he is light, dark, or black. A checker occurs when the pigeon's basic color is covered with small feathers of a darker shade—thus giving the effect of checkering. To help you understand, following is a chart showing how the colors run in the blue-color variations.

BLUE

Light-blue-bar
Regular-blue-bar (medium blue)
Blue-bar with blue rump
Blue-bar with white rump
Dark-blue-bar or smoky-blue
Barless blue (comes in all color varieties above)

This cock is a blue check of the Huysken Van Riel strain. AU 60 UTN 5370 has a No. 10 eye and is an excellent breeder.

This cock is a dark-(blue) check. Another Huysken Van Riel with a No. 10 eye, AU 67 LC 194 is proof that late hatches make good breeders.

CHECKERS

Light-blue-check
Blue-check
Medium-dark-check
Dark-check
Black-check
Solid-black
Smoky-blue-check
All of the above color varieties come in splashes and pieds.

When examining all checkers you will find that the basic or ground color is blue. In some blues and blue-checks, the basic color has a slight reddish cast to it. This is why scientists believe that the red feathering was brought into existence through years of careful breeding.

Red

Red is the second most important color, and although it is not so popular as blue, there have been many champion pigeons of the red variety. Many arguments have risen about the reliability of the red-colors when it comes to racing, but experience has shown that there is no difference between the race performances of red and blue pigeons. The reason fanciers feel that red is inferior to blue is that fewer red birds are kept, thus making the majority of winners in the blue category. If the facts were known about the percentage of red pigeons hatched as compared with blue, you would find that the *percentage* of winners runs the same.

It is also true that fanciers will take a dislike to different color varieties and will not give any such variety a fair chance. To such a fancier, all pigeons of that color variety are automatically poor racers—yet the truth of the matter is that it is the fancier's own personal taste. When starting in pigeons, do not listen to fanciers about color varieties, but treat each one with equal respect and you will find that all colors are capable of becoming champions.

The red color in a pigeon is not the bright red such as crimson or vermilion which occurs in some birds. It is more of a light chestnut-red or a light reddish-brown. Genetically, reds come in two categories: dominant red and recessive red. A dominant red cock, mated to a blue or blue-checkered hen will produce mostly red offspring, while a recessive red cock mated to a blue or blue-checkered hen will give you mostly blue or blue-checkered youngsters. This is a good way to determine the value of a red breeder. With most breeders, if the youngsters take after one or the other parent at random and none of the youngsters fly well, you can almost be sure that the dominant breeder is of no value. Only if all the offspring fail to fly well and they have one particular parent's color, can you be sure which parent is to blame.

This champion is a red-check splash (Havenith-Huysken Van Riel-Vande Wattyne-Vander Espt cross). IF 67 HPC 1646 is a winner at up to 250 miles and the sire of three winners. A widowhood cock, he has green eyes.

On the other hand, a breeder that is recessive in its color may very often be the dominant factor in the youngster's racing ability. For instance, a male or hen may be recessive in its physical (color-determining) genes, but all the youngsters of that pair *fly well*. If the color-dominant breeder has proven to produce poor-flying youngsters, then it is the pigeon that is recessive in physical-appearance genes that is dominant in the racing ability of its offspring.* So do not confuse yourself by connecting color and racing ability to the issue of recessiveness versus dominance. They are two different matters.

The experience of a Pittsburgh fancier illustrates this vividly: This fancier had a solid red cock that produced winners with any

---

*I have found this to be true from 21 years of keeping racing pigeons—and 21 years' worth of careful breeding records confirm this conclusion.

hen that was mated to him. All color varieties flew exceptionally well *except the solid reds.* In almost every case the solid red youngsters, although poor racers, would make exceptional breeders. Even at 10 years of age, Au 52 Mck 527 solid red was still producing 500- and 600-mile winners. This pigeon was one of the finest breeders ever to be produced in the Pittsburgh area and he was definitely recessive in his color. On the other hand, a good example of a pigeon that passed on his flying ability only when his color genes were dominant is the red-checkered cock that bred many red-checkered winners, but whose offspring of other colors failed completely.

As you can see, this all can be very complicated. Moreover, there are always exceptions. Therefore, all too often the genetic rule will work out in regard to color, but must be completely eliminated when it comes to racing ability. As repeated many times before, the importance of keeping correct racing and breeding records cannot be emphasized enough. This is the only way to be sure of *what is correct for your loft.*

Red pigeons have the same type patterns in their feathers as do blues. The only difference is that the patterns are red. Following is a chart of the most common red-color varieties:

Silver:	Marked exactly as the blue-bar: only the wings are yellowish-brown and the bars are red.
Dun:	The same as a silver, only a darker shade.
Mealy:	A mealy is often called a "dun" or "silver." However, the wings, although colored similar to the dun and the silver varieties, are much darker and have a smeared effect. This may be considered the smoky-blue of the reds.
Chocolate:	The pattern is the same as in the silver and dun birds, but is chocolate or cocoa-colored.
Red-Check:	The same as a blue-check, only red in color. Although there may be different shades of red-checks, they are not broken into different categories as are the blue-checks.

Solid Red:	A pigeon being solid red in color. The red is in relation to the red-check as the black is to the blue-check, since solid red is the darkest coloring in red birds, just as black is the darkest coloring in the blues.
Plum:	A very light purple being either checkered or barred. This is often called a "mosaic."
Red Grizzle:	A red pigeon having streaks of black, or darker or lighter red, running through its entire body.

Red-color varieties also come in splashes and pieds.

The two charts given are only the basic color varieties to be found in reds and blues. There are many other varieties of these colors, but it is impossible to list them all. Besides, it takes years to learn the many different color-types of the racing pigeon.

One strange fact with the reds is that any red birds having black mixed in are always cocks.

Uncommon Colors

Many very uncommon color varieties also appear in racing pigeons. Some of these colors are a washed-out variety of a popular dominant color. These colors are drab and are sometimes described as being pastel in nature. For some unknown reason these color varieties are weak both in breeding and in flying, and it is only the exception that makes a good racer.

Sometimes birds are bred that have triple color: one wing may be red while the other is blue. But these are nothing but genetic accidents.

Some birds are solid black, like a crow, or solid white like a dove. Although these are not too common in racing pigeons, they are still available—and many make excellent flyers and breeders. If strange colors do arise out of youngsters you have bred from regular-colored pigeons, you know they are "throw-backs," and you should put special attention into finding out such a bird's value as a flyer or breeder. Never eliminate birds by color, but give them all a fair chance.

This red-check cock is a Pittsburgh Southern Combine Hall of Fame winner. AU 64 JNT 422 Red Check is proof that red coloration does not handicap a flyer.

The grizzles, although uncommon, are still very popular among fanciers. Grizzling is an uneven speckled arrangement of white on the head, neck, wing, tail, and body and also involves a distinct color pattern on the pigeon's flight feathers. These patterns are most often connected to blues and whites, but they also occur in other color varieties.* In good grizzles the head and neck have a frostlike appearance. There have been many grizzles

*The Red Grizzle was described on page 88. It is seen even less often than the other grizzle patterns.

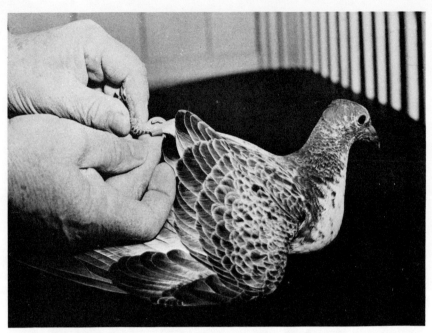

Red is the rarest of the grizzle patterns. Here someone is banding a young red grizzle with a removable plastic identification band.

that have won races and earned special spots in their masters' lofts. This color variety is quite hardy and robust.

To sum up the subject, it can only be said that there is good and bad in all colors, and that the only true way to find their worth is by flying them.

9. TEACHING THE YOUNG BIRD

Young-bird training begins on the day you band the squeaker. If it is not handled roughly, the first lesson is that its master will do it no harm. The cleaning of the nest box and the handling when checking for sickness is the beginning of learning the loft routine. The gentle whistle and the rattling of the feed-can is the beginning of the youngster's connection to sound, Man and food.

Do not feel that a young pigeon in the nest is not capable of the learning process, for it is a proven fact: birds that were hurt or scared while in the nest develop a fear of Man which they never lose. If you treat your pigeons with tender loving care, they will reward you by showing a desire to home. This desire is what wins races.

A pigeon is a slave to habit, and good habits are learned just as quickly as the bad ones. Once a pigeon learns a set pattern, it is very difficult to change his habits, whether they be good or bad.

After Weaning

Whenever the youngsters are capable of drinking, eating, and flying to a perch, it is time to train them to enter and leave the loft. All pigeons must be taught to enter upon command. They must enter upon the call to feed—for instance, a whistle or your

Many fanciers use a self-woven "pigeon-man's net" as a loft stick. The net is used, not to catch the birds, but to direct them towards the entrance of the loft. Whatever kind of loft stick you decide upon, it must be made a part of the birds' everyday existence.

rattling of the feed-can. They must also learn to enter by being driven in. You should be able to walk the pigeons into the loft at any time. Teaching both systems will assure you of complete control over your birds.

Use a specially constructed flight cage made of 1″ × 2″ galvanized wire when you are training the youngsters to enter the loft and learn their surroundings. The flight cage should be large enough to hold the entire first hatch. It should fit on the landing board in front of the traps and ought to be constructed for easy removal.

Introduce a loft stick at this time. A stick $1'' \times \frac{1}{2}''$ and $36''$ long is ideal. The four sharp edges and the ends should be rounded off so that no accidental damage can be done to the birds. Carry this stick with you at all times and touch the youngsters gently with it to show them that they have nothing to fear. Under *no* circumstances should the stick harm any of the youngsters. Upon leaving the loft, hang the stick where the birds can see it. This teaches them that the loft stick is a part of the daily routine. You will eventually use this stick in driving the birds into the loft.

You must teach the youngsters to enter and leave the loft upon command. You can accomplish this by opening the exit, setting them into the flight cage, and then giving them your call for "OUT." This may be a different-sounding whistle from the feed-whistle, or just your saying "Out boys," or some phrase like that. After all the birds are in the flight cage, go to the landing board and, through the wire, gently push them through the traps with the loft stick, making sure the signal for "IN" is given. Reward them with a little treat, preferably pigeon candy. This process must be repeated until the youngsters can exit and enter without any help.

During the day leave the traps open so the youngsters can enter and exit into the flight cage. In this way they learn the surrounding area. When you find that they have learned to enter and exit, it is then time to remove the flight cage.

Do not wait until the youngsters are strong in the wings to teach them to sit on the landing board without the flight cage. Pick a calm, clear day and in late afternoon let them out without the aid of the flight cage. Do not chase them out, but just open the traps and let them come out on their own. Pick a spot by the landing board to stand. You should use this spot at all times so the youngsters become accustomed to your presence on the outside. At this time be very careful that nothing scares them: stay by the landing board, slowly walking in front and making sure that the loft stick is present at all times. Your birds must have as much faith in you outside the loft as they do inside.

The whole time the youngsters are on the landing board, talk to them and touch them with your hand and the loft stick. When it is time to feed, gently push them through the traps with the aid of your hand and stick, making sure the feed-call is given. The stubborn birds that do not enter should not be fed that day. Do not worry, because the loss of one meal will not hurt them. Under no circumstances should you feed the birds that did not listen.

Repeat this process daily, weather permitting, until you have full control of your team of youngsters. Trapping should be taught early because a wing-strong pigeon knows that he can get away from you. Once he develops the bad habit of disobeying, his bad ways may eventually teach the others to do the same. For this reason a persistent youngster should be destroyed.

The First Flight

If you have trained the youngsters properly, the first flight should not be dangerous. As the youngsters get stronger, they become braver by flapping their wings and rising a few feet into the air. As their strength increases, so does the length of time they stay in the air. They may take a few fast circles round the loft, and as the days go by these flights become longer.

Flocking

Eventually you will find the entire flock flying about in as many different directions as there are pigeons. Although flocking is a natural instinct, the pigeon still has to learn it. For days, and possibly weeks, your young-bird team will fly about in all directions, darting about and dive-bombing through the trees. Eventually you will see a couple of birds flying together, and as days go by the number increases until the entire flock is flying together.

Do not let your pigeons get into the habit of landing on roofs. *Teach them to land only on the landing board.* Do not throw stones at the nearby roofs, but have a rubber ball with a string attached, to use in chasing the birds. Any pigeon that persists in landing on the roof should be destroyed, no matter how valuable you feel he is. It takes only one bird with bad habits to completely disorganize your entire flock.

Tripping

Tripping has always been the Number One cause of loss of youngsters. Young pigeons love to fly, and very often these flights take them many miles away from home and are hours in duration. So very often the weaker youngsters fall behind and are lost.

Every year you will hear fanciers talking about losing all or part of their young-bird team because of a FLYAWAY. This phenomenon is unexplainable: only theories have been given to try to explain what happens. The most common theory is that the youngsters go into a flying frenzy: they fly and fly until exhaustion overcomes them. One by one the flock gets smaller as the weaker pigeons begin to drop out. Only the strongest are able to make it back to the loft, while the remainder are scattered for miles, landing on houses, trees, wires or any other spot that their tired wings sit them.

For days after, the stragglers will wander in, but many will never return. What happens to these pigeons will never be known—some may stray to other lofts, while others may fall to predators, accidents and even death through starvation. This is truly a heart-breaking experience, but maybe it can be prevented:

If the youngsters were taught from the earliest possible age to recognize the loft, landing board, and surrounding area, their mental powers will be advanced. If the young birds' muscles were developed before their learning ability, you can be certain of heavy losses. Pigeons are no different from any other form of life in that they must be taught and *taught correctly*.

Do not crowd the youngsters, for overcrowding will lead to heavier losses, sickness and failure. For some strange reason, the larger flocks trip longer and more often than the smaller flocks. This may be caused by the large flocks' discontent at overcrowding and unhealthy conditions.

Let youngsters out only when they are in a hungry condition. This ensures better control over them and takes away some of their desire to trip. Late afternoon flights are best with only occasional mid-morning or afternoon flights. As the young birds mature, they may occasionally be let out in the morning.

Remember that on Saturdays and Sundays, races and training-tosses are being held, so this increases the flocks of pigeons which may influence your youngsters to fly away.

Do not think about training young birds for the races until the entire young flock has learned all loft procedures. All pigeons should enter the loft when you indicate, either by driving or calling, that you want them. Moreover, they should be flocking well, staying aloft for long periods of time, and landing only on the landing board.

Any pigeon that persists in disobeying should be disposed of. Do not fool yourself into believing that this rebel is worth saving: he will only give you many hours of aggravation.

10. COOPIES

Many fanciers use different breeds of pigeons in aiding their racers to land and trap faster. Many races have been lost because of a pigeon that would not land upon returning from a race. To help bring the bird down quickly, use a coopie (a coop bird), which can be seen from quite a distance.

Coopies or Decoy Birds

The coop bird also has the unique quality of not flying well—one or two turns about the loft is about all it can handle and then it lands. The coopie can also be trained to fly a few feet right to the landing board and rush into the trap, hopefully bringing the race bird down with it.

Keep the coop bird with the flyers so they become used to it. And use the coop bird on training-tosses so that both the coopie and the flyers become familiar with this procedure. If you use the coopie on race-days and the flyer is not accustomed to seeing it, the coopie's appearance may lead to more lost time. Treat the coopie in the strictest way. Following is a short description of the most common coopies.

Oriental Frills

The Satinette is the most popular of the coop birds. It belongs to the Oriental Frill family, which was developed in Smyrna,

Most popular of all the coop birds are the Satinettes.

Turkey, and became extremely popular when introduced in England and Germany about 1864.

All Satinettes have frills on the breast and have feathers on their legs and feet. This kind of appearance is called "grouse-muffed." On the back of their heads Satinettes have a peak that turns upwards, pointing toward the front of the pigeon. Their beaks are very short and hooked, resembling a parakeet beak. In fact, the beak is so short that many Satinettes are unable to' feed their own youngsters, and Satinette squabs must be raised by the homing pigeon or other varieties having longer beaks.

The most stunning characteristic of the Satinette is the exquisite shades of soft pastel colors and beautiful lace patterns

This decoy bird is a Satinette of the Dun-laced Blondinette variety.

that occur on its wings. No other breed of pigeons has such beautiful colors and patterns. The Satinettes come in many different color varieties: Sulpherettes, Brunettes, Bluettes, Blondinettes, Vizors, Silverettes, Black-and-Dun-laced Satinettes, Black-and-Dun-laced Blondinettes, Dominoes, and Barred Blondinettes. There are also color variations of each color variety.

The only big drawback with Satinettes is that the male has a tendency to be a bit scrappy and often has been known to scalp* a youngster that has fallen to the floor. Nest Satinettes in the highest possible nest so they have less chance to spend time on the floor—and thus fewer opportunities to attack fallen youngsters.

*Scalping is the name given to an older pigeon's attack on a youngster whenever the older pigeon pecks away at the youngster until the feathers and the top layer of skin have been completely torn from the youngster's head.

Schietti Modenas seldom have white plumage. This coopie has just won a prize in show competition.

Modenas

The Modena is one of the oldest known pigeon varieties to be in existence today. It originated in Modena, Italy, about 2,000 years ago, and it was not until 1884 that it was introduced into Germany and England.

There are 152 different color varieties of the Modena Pigeon. These "coopies" are divided into two groups: the *Gazzi* and the *Schietti*. The *Gazzi* has a white body with only its head, bib, wings and tail being colored. The *Schietti* is colored the same; however, it lacks the white body of the *Gazzi*.

The Modena's body is very short and stubby; the wings and tail are also very short. When standing, a Modena will give you the impression that it is trying to stand on its toes. It has a short beak and a round, erect head that continuously bobs about. The entire bird is built very compact, and this build gives the Modena the impression of being a round ball.

Although the males have a tendency to fight, it is very rare to see one attack a youngster. They are very good parents and are able to raise their own young.

Helmets

The Helmet is a variety of the German Tumbler and in appearance it resembles a Nun. It is a very small bird, being only half the size of a racer. Helmets are entirely white, except for their tails and the tops of their heads. (This color on top of the pigeon's head is what gives this variety its name.) The back of this pigeon's head has a tuft of feathers which may run from ear to ear and swirl forwards. The Helmet is a shy bird and only on rare occasions will he fight with a racer.

Strassers are raised mainly for food and show, but fanciers have found that they also make good coopies. Note the resemblance of this blue-barred Strasser hen to the Gazzi-Modena feather pattern.

You will find that some coopies will fly more than you want them to. You can correct this by clipping its wings. Clip the wings according to how well the bird is able to fly. Cut only one primary flight at a time and test the coopie on how well he tosses. Keep clipping only one flight at a time until the bird is able to fly to the landing board with ease, but is unable to stay in the air for more than one or two circles.

A wise fancier always keeps a few coopies by his side in a small basket so he can reach in and release one should he feel that his returning race bird is hesitating to land.

The Helmet, a shy bird, will do his best to avoid fights in your loft. Here, a banded coopie.

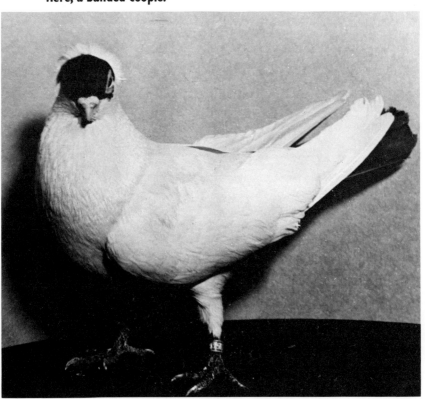

Helmets also come with grouse legs. If you find that your coopie flies too far, clip its wings—but just one flight at a time.

When obtaining your coopies, it is advisable to buy only coop birds of high quality. Not only are they prettier and more robust, but they also seem to have a higher intelligence. There is a big demand for good coopies, and you may be able to sell or trade any youngsters that you might raise.

II. YOUNG-BIRD RACING

Only pigeons that are banded in the same year as the young-bird season are eligible to fly those particular races. (If banded in 1972 they are eligible to fly only the 1972 young-bird series.) These youngsters are to be your future old birds, so take as much time as possible to train them correctly. If not trained properly as a young bird, your pigeon will never become a good old bird.

The United States is more interested in flying young birds than is any other country in the world. It has been only in recent years that Europeans have shown an increased interest in flying young birds.

Some fanciers make young birds their specialty and every year they manage to win more than their share of the young-bird races. Most old-bird experts claim that winning with young birds is more luck than knowledge. However, this statement has been disproven because of certain flyers who win consistently. There is much to learn if you want to be successful with young birds: the following pages will help you succeed.

Carrying Crates

Most pigeon crates are made from buff, willow, or canvas. These pigeon crates come in various shapes and sizes. You may construct your own or purchase some from your local pigeon-supply dealer. Very often a local flyer makes and sells them to make a little extra money.

This carrying crate is an excellent type to ship your flyers in. Make sure that the young birds are thoroughly familiar with the carrying crate before you take them on their first training-toss.

It is always best to have the crate a little larger than the number of pigeons enclosed requires, since overcrowding can lead to broken flight feathers and other injuries. You will need more than one crate, and be sure that no crate is too large to handle easily or too large to fit into the back of the car. *Do not put pigeons into the trunk or boot of your car.* The risk of their smothering is too great.

Another very useful type of basket is the partition type. This crate is made up into many different compartments, each large enough to handle only one bird. It is used mainly by widow-hood flyers.

Construct the crates so that they are easy to clean and store them away when you are not using them. Clean the crates at least once a week during racing season. Cedar chips or Stay-Dri are the two best media to use in the bottom of the crates.

Training the Young Bird

Before you begin basket-training your youngsters, the entire flock of young birds must be flocking and must be flying for long

Overcrowding can result in broken flight feathers and other injuries that ruin your birds' racing performances. Make sure that your pigeons have plenty of room in the carrying crate (as shown above).

lengths of time. Moreover, they should have started tripping and must know all loft procedures. If you flight-train young birds that are not ready mentally, expect only heavy losses: If a young pigeon is too young or too dumb to learn loft procedures, how can you expect him to find his way home from miles away?

Three or four weeks before the races begin you must start training your birds. Young birds are very excitable, so proceed with caution. They must first be accustomed to being placed into the training basket [that is, the crate]. Catch all the birds and place them in the baskets, then take them outside and let them sit on the lawn for at least a half an hour. This gives them time to calm down and get used to the crates. After they have calmed down, release them one at a time. Do not coax them out but let them find the opening by themselves. This will teach them how to get out on their own. As soon as they land they must be driven into the loft. Use the loft stick and give the IN-signal. Feed them immediately after they have entered and make sure that the stragglers do not get fed. Repeat this process at least two more times, making sure that all birds leave the crate on their own. Write down the band numbers of the birds that are slow to learn or listen.

Before you start down the road, plan how and where to train. Get two maps, one of your local area in detail and one that shows the whole area from your loft to the first race-station in your locality. Draw a straight line from the race-station to your town and mark all important towns and routes between these two points. Since pigeons do not fly in a straight line, but in an arc, it is advisable to get past race results and mark the locations of the winning lofts on the maps. Once you have marked these locations, it is easy to see in what direction most of the winning pigeons live, and you must train in that direction. Once a pigeon has been taught to come from a certain direction, it forms a flying pattern and on race-day it has a tendency to come from this direction.

The point is: if you are training on the line (from what you think is the shortest distance) and the race birds are arcing to the north (or south or so on), your birds will have a tendency to backtrack: that is, to overfly or go off course to their familiar training grounds before they fly home to the loft. And in this way your birds lose many valuable minutes—sometimes they are even hours behind.

Many short tosses are advisable in training young birds. These short tosses teach the birds more than they could learn from just a few long trips. The pigeon has the homing ability: it is up to *you* to develop it. These short tosses teach your pigeon what is expected of him—and once this has been learned, the distances may be increased. *Do not be in a hurry to catch up to the other fanciers.* Through experience, those fanciers who are always in a hurry to get to great distances lose many pigeons.

Stay in the first training spot until you see that *all* your birds are in a hurry to leave the crates and that they head straight for home. Your training schedule may be worked out as follows:

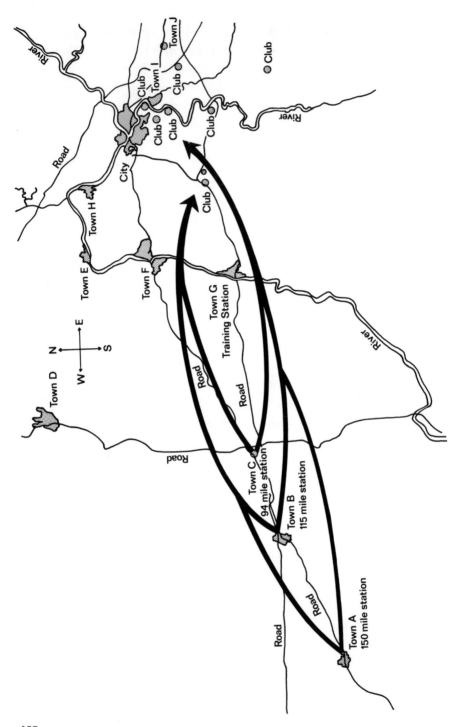

four tosses at 1 mile, four at 2 miles, four at 5 miles, four at 15 miles, two at 20 miles, and one at 50 miles. Once 50 miles has been reached the birds are capable of flying a short race. Moreover, after your birds have successfully made the 50-mile run, you do not have to continuously give them 50-mile tosses. Any distance between the loft and 50 miles is sufficient, so long as your pigeons are on the line of flight (the direction that the winning race birds come from). If the birds are exercising well about the loft, then two 50-mile tosses and as many short ones as possible are sufficient. There are three forms of training: single-, flock- and van-tosses. Each works equally well, with the choice being up to your personal discretion.

Single-Toss

In single-tossing, a fancier will release each bird separately and will not release another until the first one is out of sight. If at all possible, release your pigeons from a high point and watch through binoculars to make sure that each bird is well on its way before you release another. This type of training teaches the bird to fly by itself *and to break from the flock on race-days*. A big drawback with this type of training is that it consumes much time if done correctly.

At this stage, do not worry about the time your pigeons take in returning home, because pigeons have a tendency to hang about waiting for another pigeon. Patience must be shown—and, besides, all birds must be forced to home by themselves. While training, take notes on each bird you release: mark down the time the bird took to leave the crate, if it flew high or low, how much zip was in its take-off, and how much desire it showed in wanting to leave.

It is best if someone can drive the birds in when they arrive from the training-toss. This teaches them fast trapping and also to expect to see somebody waiting for them upon their return.

The line of flight to the home loft may not always be a straight line: it may well be a gentle arc that bends in the direction of the prevailing winds. The breaking point is somewhere along the line of flight.

Your pigeons should be rewarded by being fed at the end of each training-toss.

Flock-Tossing

Flock-tossing is the most common practice. Every pigeon is released at once, and this simulates racing conditions. When flock-tossing you will find that your pigeons leave the release-area much faster and head straight for home. The biggest advantage is the amount of time saved.

Some fanciers do not release all of their pigeons at once, but release the birds in several small flocks. If you have 40 youngsters, release them in five flocks of 8 birds, the theory being that the race birds do not come home in one large flock. Just as when you are single-tossing, arrange for someone to be at home to drive the pigeons into the loft immediately upon their arrival.

Van-Tosses

Almost every area has somebody who trains birds by taking them for training-tosses. It is extremely wise of you to use this training van as much as possible. Van-tosses have the same effect on the pigeon as a race does: for a training van will have hundreds of pigeons from many different lofts and will mix them all up and thus force the pigeons to find their ways home without the aid of a loft-mate. This may be one of the best ways to prepare your pigeons for the races.

It is also cheaper and it saves time and wear on your car. It also frees you, so that you yourself can drive the pigeons in as they return home and can mark their band numbers down. (You do this to keep records on which birds are training best.)

Two van-tosses a week plus a few shorter tosses may be enough to put your youngsters into racing condition.

Exercising about the Loft

After training has begun you will find that the youngsters' desire to exercise about the loft is greatly reduced. If the pigeons are training well, are in top condition and not heavy, you will find that they still love to fly but the tripping will have

A big advantage of the van-toss is that it approximates actual racing conditions.

ceased. When the team is lazy and refuses to fly then you know something is wrong. If your birds are not ill, then probably they are overweight—or some other lack of condition is the reason they are reluctant to fly.

Another reason why birds will not fly as long as they should is that they are sent out of the loft in a very hungry state. As noted before, youngsters should be kept a little on the hungry side—but never to the point where they are desperate for food.

A healthy pigeon in condition is naturally active and peppy and should always be anxious to leave the loft for its two daily exercises. As your pigeons rise to the air they should give the impression of great strength and speed.

Flagging as an Exercise Control

Many flyers use the FLAGGING SYSTEM to keep their birds in the air for specific lengths of time. You accomplish this by attaching a flag to a long pole and placing it close to the landing board. This keeps the birds from landing until the allotted exercise time is up—at which time you remove the flag.

You may feel that flagging will unduly upset the birds. This is not so, because pigeons manage to separate what their owners do outside the loft from what the owners do inside. The big drawback is that few fanciers have the time to ensure that the birds are exercising properly the whole time the flag is up, and many birds get wise to this and land on a house until it is time to be called in.* When you observe pigeons that are being flagged, you may notice that they are moving their wings without any effort and are scarcely exerting themselves. If so, this form of exercise is a waste of time, and it would be better to take the time used in flagging to run the birds down the road for a flight home.

Lazy Pigeons

In many lofts where the birds are not exercising correctly, there are often a few lazy birds that are causing the entire flock to land prematurely. If you watch the birds carefully, it will not take you long to find the guilty parties. In checking your training records, you will find that these same birds are always late. These birds will never make a champion—all they are capable of doing is slowing down the rest of your flock. Do not show mercy on these stragglers but eliminate them from your loft.

*Moreover, if adopted, the flagging system must be used morning and evening and, for best results, the fancier must be there 100 per cent of the time while flagging. A workingman may find it difficult to fulfil these two conditions.

Feeding Young-Bird Racers

How to feed young birds is most important, not only for the general health of the youngsters but also for endurance, a good moult, and their speed in trapping. Youngsters must be fed a variety of top-quality grains if they are to obtain the necessary development to fly well, stay in condition, and proceed normally with the moult.

The feeding of race birds could be described as an art. It is an art that many fanciers will never learn because of their lack of experience and defective sense of observation.

It does not hurt to let the youngsters stay a little on the heavy side while being trained. But now that the races are approaching, all fat and excess weight must be eliminated. Where fanciers go wrong is that they force their youngsters to lose weight by cutting their feed to the point of near-starvation. The birds must be fed so that their muscles contain no fat, yet they must be fed enough to keep those muscles firm and supple. The art of feeding is in giving the youngsters enough to sustain them in good condition but leaving the impression on the bird that it did not receive enough.

The importance of a high-quality feed is to replace the lost energy caused by exercise, to supplement the needs of growing youngsters, to re-build the tissues of exhausted race birds, and to give reserve energy for a proper moult.

Some fanciers count the exact number of grains per bird, some weigh the amount per bird, or even measure or weigh the amounts per flock, but these systems do not take into consideration that the amount needed varies greatly from day to day. This is why it may be best to hand-feed. With this system you feed handfuls at a time until your birds start going for water. As soon as they start this, do not feed any more until all the grains are completely cleaned up and then give them a small amount of pigeon candy. (Pigeon candy consists of small seeds that are high in oil content: such as linseed, canary seed or the seeds of rape, hemp, and anise.)

Keep a careful check on the youngsters' weight. If you find them too thin, then increase the amount given; if they are heavy, cut the amount or give them more roadwork or exercise about the loft.

You must remember one thing: if young birds are stunted, fed improperly, flown hard, or permitted to suffer any other set-back, they will not make good old birds. The body tissues will have been damaged at an early age and these tissues can never be replaced.

Greens, except lettuce, may be given to young birds on Mondays. Grit should be given *daily* so that they get the proper amount of minerals. Water should always be clean and plentiful.

Keep a separate notebook for racing. In this book, list all band numbers, colors, and parentages. The race-stations, distances, and race schedules should also be included for easy reference. Every week write down the birds shipped, the body form, and the condition of the moult. You should also record all pools and expenditures for future reference.

On race-day mark down the weather and wind speed at the release-point, the time your youngsters are released and the weather conditions and wind speed at home. Upon arrival, the birds' times, band numbers and your birds' general reactions should be recorded. You should keep track of any birds that trap badly, circle too long, or jump off the landing board when approached. This is often just a nervous reaction, but if you find that it is a habit with certain birds, then either work with these birds separately or eliminate them completely.

Only birds that are training well should be considered for the races. Youngsters that are a little slow and have not mastered all procedures should be given consideration and trained more before you enter them in a race.

When you are picking birds, the condition of the moult must be taken into consideration. The loss of the small feathers on the head and particularly those about the ears gives the bird a large handicap. Do not ship any birds that are in this moult condition because you will lose many of them. Pigeons that are moulting their covert feathers (the small feathers that overlap the second-aries and primaries) should not be shipped, either. These covert feathers not only protect the flight feathers from rain, but they moreover lend support to them during flight. Do not worry about the loss of a few tail feathers, because many young birds have won races with a heavy tail moult. However, it may be advisable not to send your pigeon to the *longer* races if it is in a heavy tail moult.

After this, check the flight feathers. It is obvious that if a pigeon is to do its best, it should not be handicapped by the absence of its outer wing flights. If a flight feather falls before the one next to it is fully grown, it causes a large gap in the wing. Naturally this retards the bird's flight and is a big strain on the

Corky "like a tennis ball," this blue-check hen (AU 71 SWC 1837) has won combine prizes in races up to 207 miles.

pigeon. It would be advisable to keep any bird home that has more than one flight out of a wing. For races, pick birds with flight feathers that are partially grown or have just been dropped. Take great care with your birds when they have dropped the eighth, ninth, or tenth flight, because with some birds the dropping of these flights causes a soreness in the wing. Ship only when these flights are half grown and the tenderness is gone.

Weight is the next factor to take into consideration: do not ship any birds that are overly fat. Birds that are a *little* heavy may be shipped to give them race experience, and often you may be lucky enough to place high in the standings with one of these. The well-conditioned pigeon will be light in weight and give you the impression that he is made from cork. Many fanciers describe this as "being like a tennis ball."

Once you have chosen your entries, it is time to nominate them for the pools. This is best done by checking your training records and listing the most consistent pigeons.* From these birds, pick the ones in best condition and pool them accordingly. The birds of lesser consistency should be pooled the least.

The Day Before the Race

The day before a race it sometimes helps to give the birds a small training-toss. Do not make it a long distance where they may become tired, but just far enough to tone up the muscles. After they return, feed them lightly and do not disturb them until it is time to feed again. Be very careful that nothing excites them before the race. In deciding what birds to ship, give yourself enough time to go through the pigeons thoroughly: do not wait until the last second and rush through them, as, this way, you increase your chances of making improper choices.

Never send birds to the race without feeding them. You should give a light feeding 3 hours before the birds are crated. At this time, make sure, too, that they get a drink of water.

---

*A consistent pigeon is not necessarily a constant winner but it is one that constantly gives a good account of itself: in other words, it is always one of the first home from both the races and the training-tosses.

Another prime-condition hen, AU 71 SWC 1816 has placed high in both club and combine races although she has flown in only six races. 1816 is a medium-check of the Huysken Van Riel strain.

The Race

The birds are now taken to the clubhouse where they are all crated together, prior to being released for the race. First though, each bird is officially banded with a temporary race band called a COUNTERMARK, which is placed on his leg. This countermark is made of rubber and has numbers printed on both the outside and inside. A slip of paper with corresponding numbers comes with each countermark. The bird's band number is written on this slip of paper by a clubhouse official, and the paper is placed in a

A typical scene just before liberation. The clubhouse officials are in charge now.

sealed envelope. The countermark number must correspond to the slip of paper, in order for the outcome of the race to be accurately checked.

After the countermarking, you must fill out the entry sheets and give them to the Race Secretary. Then you pay the shipping charges. When picking up your clock, check to see if it is running and make sure that it corresponds to the master timer. Make sure, too, that the seal is on properly and that the Number One hole is showing in the capsule slot. Always keep your timer in a safe place.

The pigeons are now placed in the shipping crates and are transported to the point of liberation. Early in the morning, weather permitting, all birds are liberated together and they head for home and their waiting owners.

When you are waiting for the pigeons to return, everything should be the same as on a training-toss. Stand in the same location, wear the same type of clothing, use the same coopie and have your loft stick ready. Since pigeons are generally nervous upon returning from a race, you should show only calmness. It may be hard not to show excitement, but remember, many races have been lost because a pigeon was scared back into the air by the fancier's overanxiousness in clocking.

Very often a flock of race birds may pass over your loft. Whenever this happens, immediately give a whistle and throw the coop bird because quite often pigeons (especially young birds) may stick with the flock and be a little hesitant in dropping out.

If one of your birds is in the flock, your call and the tossing of the coop bird will draw him out.

When your bird lands, drive it into the traps, making sure that you do not make any sudden movements to scare it back into the air. Remove the countermark from the bird's leg and place it into a metal capsule that you are then to place into the top of the clock. Finally, turn the key. The time of the bird's arrival is stamped on a piece of rolled clock paper, with the exact hour, minute and second recorded. The number of birds clocked is governed by the club that you belong to: some set a limit, and others let you clock as many as you want.

After the race, feed the birds that have raced only a mixture of small grains. A light feeding helps the pigeon's digestive system to rest after such a strenuous ordeal as a race.

When you have clocked your quota, take the clock to the club so the speed of your birds may be figured. (See Chapter 12 on The Club). Do not forget to be a good sport and congratulate the winner if you lose.

After the Race

For the rest of the day the birds should be left to rest. The evening feeding should also contain only the smaller grains. Do not resume their regular mixture until the next day. Monday should also be used as a rest day. After their morning flight, feed the birds and give them their weekly bath, using lukewarm water to relax their muscles. You may add a pinch of potassium permanganate to the bath water as a preventative against germs or insect pests that they may have picked up in the race from some less careful fancier's pigeons.

Tuesday is the beginning of the pigeon's work-week, and the daily routine goes back to normal. All exercising and loft routine must continue the same as it did previously. Do not make any changes: any experimental changes in the middle of a race season may throw your entire team out of condition. Use the winter months to plan your changes and then do them at the beginning of a race season, but never in the middle. The only time any changes should be made is if something is drastically wrong and the change will correct the situation.

12. THE CLUB

Every country has federations that are responsible for the organization and administration of the sport. These federations help in establishing the rules and by-laws that are a guideline to the clubs. Most clubs are self-governing and use the federations' by-laws only as a guide. New clubs must apply for a charter if they want to belong to a federation, and it is always best to belong to a large federation because of the many benefits that it brings.

The club officers in America consist of a President, Vice-President, Secretary–Treasurer, Race Secretary, and the committee. The committee should have more control in running the club than any one member, and items of great importance should be voted on by the body.

Each club draws up a set of by-laws that govern the conduct of the club and its members. These by-laws govern such subjects as dues, voting, duties of officers, membership, resignations, boundaries of the club, procedure of the meetings, and any other item of importance.

Besides the by-laws, a set of race rules must be drawn up, to be abided by at all times; and any deviation from these will lead to disqualification from the race. These race rules should be learned by every member so there are no misunderstandings.

In most areas the different clubs merge to form a combine. The most important function of the combine is to obtain cheaper and better forms of transportation for the birds. Instead of each club's having its own transportation, the various clubs combine to ship together and have one large liberation. The combine has its own set of rules and often awards diplomas and trophies for placing high in combine competition. This adds interest in the combine and makes competition much keener.

All laws are made to protect the members, to benefit everyone, and to protect them from the dishonest. It is sad to think that any dishonesty is connected with racing pigeons, but as with anything else there are always a few "rotten apples."

All novices should be informed that they are expected to help in the running of the club. Every member should have at least one duty to perform on transporting night or on race-day, even if it is just helping with the crating of the birds, their counter-marking, or simply cleaning up. *The work load should not be left for just a few members.* No matter how small the job, every bit of help makes the club run smoother.

The Clock

The correct setting of the race clock is most important in having the correct speed on race-day. Even though most clubs have a clock committee, it is advisable to learn to set your own clock, so that you have an understanding of how it works.

There are many different kinds of timers on the market, with the standard printing clock being the most used. The most common clock used in the United States and Britain is the Benzing continuous timer [Comatic]. It is easy to obtain, keeps good time and is easy to use.

In setting a timer, begin by sliding the bolt back to open the lid. This releases the two locking devices inside the lid. When you close the lid, a little hole is punched in the tape. Check this every race-day to make sure only one hole was punched.

After the lid is opened, wind the clock with the clock-crank or double-ended key. There is a small lever on the front end of the timer. Move this to the left; this stops the clock when the second hand reaches zero. Next, find the drum or metal disc where the capsules are placed and lift it off its spindle. Remove

Close-up of a Benzing Comatic: the bird is clocked by your dropping a capsule containing his countermark into the Benzing's timer.

the glass covering on the clock face. You set the hour hand with the aid of a key and push the minute hand to the time that has been set for starting. The glass is then replaced and then the clock is started according to the master time. If your timer was set for 6:30, it is started when the master timer reaches 6:30.

Always make sure that there is enough paper in the clock. Turn the brass drum cover until the Number One hole is showing. Now replace the drum. When you do this, make sure that the drum is centered on the striking key spindle. The clock is then closed and sealed with the club's wire clock-seal.

Make sure it has been set correctly to the master timer, that it is running, and the Number One hole is showing.

After all the birds have been clocked, all clocks must be checked at the clubhouse and the speeds must be figured. The clock-seal is checked to make sure that the seal number corresponds with the master sheet. Then the seal is cut off. A time is noted from the master timer, and the clock is struck at this time, thus stamping the cut-off time. The clock is then opened, and clubhouse officials or the clock committee figure each bird's speed.

Figuring a Race

All active pigeon-flyers must have airline distances before they are able to fly. The loft must be surveyed by the club Secretary, and the measurements are sent to an accredited surveyor so he may figure accurate airline measurements. These airlines give the distance from the liberation point to the loft, figured to the thousandths of a mile. This means that on the 300-mile station your pigeon may fly 307.431 miles.

After the clocks are opened and the paper tapes are removed, the countermarks are checked and listed on the report sheet in the order that the pigeons were clocked.

The next step is to read the tapes and list in rotation the clocking time, noting the last stop-time. If there is any difference between the last stamping-time and the master time, it must be adjusted. If the clock was running slow, the time is added; if it was running fast, the time is deducted. If you clocked at 12:01:01 and your clock is 2 minutes fast according to the master time, this makes the correct timing of the pigeon at 11:59:01.

The liberation time is then noted: if the birds were liberated at 6:30 A.M. and clocked at 11:59:01, you know that the bird was on the wing for 5 hours, 29 minutes and 1 second. Through the aid of a special chart, the actual flying time is reduced to seconds: thus the bird flew 19,741 seconds. The airline distance is reduced to yards by multiplying by 1,760 (yards per mile) and then is multiplied by 60 to reduce it to 60th's of a yard. The number of seconds is divided into the number of 60th's of a yard, and this will give the speed in yards per minute. These calculations are made on an electric calculator that makes figuring the speeds quite simple.

At the end of the year, each fancier's speeds of each race are combined and the average speed is figured out to determine the best flyer in the club for that season. The speeds of each club's winner is submitted to the combine Secretary, and he figures the combine's Grand Champion.

To win Average Speed in a club is a great distinction, but to win Combine Average brings you twice the esteem. You know that all your hard work paid off and that through much skill and patience the pigeons showed their love for home by crowning their master Grand Champion.

Benzing Comatic with the lid removed: make sure, every race-day, that only one hole is punched in the tape when you close the lid.

13. OLD-BIRD RACING

The date that you select for mating the old-bird flyers will be influenced by the starting date of the first old-bird race. The first round of youngsters must be weaned and the old-bird flyers should be down on their second round of eggs at least seven days before the first race. The first flight should have been dropped, showing that the bird is in proper physical and mental health.

Training Your Old Birds

After the long winter many birds have become fat, and their muscles are soft and flabby. During mating and the rearing of youngsters much weight has been lost, but the muscles still remain soft. This is corrected by daily exercise and as the muscles begin to develop again, the exercise should be increased. Do not force the pigeons to fly for long periods of time until you are sure that the muscles and respiratory system have been brought back into form.

About 3 or 4 weeks before the first race the birds should be given their first training-toss. A 2-mile toss is ideal for the first time: this gives the old bird a chance to revive his homing instincts without making him work too hard. Give at least six 5-mile tosses. Continue these frequent short tosses until you see that the birds are hurrying home. Once your pigeons have

"Young Patrick," a Belgian champion, took fourth prize in the Poitiers race (500-1,000 miles) as a young-bird flyer and, just a year later, first prize in the Chateauroux long-distance race.

remembered what is expected of them, you may increase the distances. The training-tosses may then jump to 10 miles, then 15, 20, 40—and then to the short races.

Although old birds have experience in racing, it is not advisable to rush them. It is wise to train them with caution. After raising, training, flying them as young birds, and feeding them through the winter, why throw them away because of over-anxiousness?

The big difficulty in training old birds is that the cocks and hens have to be trained separately if they are on eggs or have small youngsters. One parent must be left at home to tend the nest. Not until the youngsters are fully feathered are they able to spend the cool days or nights unattended.

Many fanciers raise only one youngster to a nest on the first round—this includes both the flyers and the breeders. This enables the youngsters to be moved from the flyers to the breeders until the flyers return from the training-toss. The youngsters are then returned to their own nests. Take care that the youngsters are not mixed up in the process of moving them: write each move down; do not rely on your memory.

If the eggs under the flyers are not to be hatched, dummy eggs should be used. Dummy eggs are wooden or glass eggs that are used to replace the fertile pigeon eggs when hatching is not desired. They are used up to the day of hatching. On the eighteenth day a newly hatched youngster from the breeders should be placed under the flyers so their breeding cycle will continue normally.

It is best to let them feed this youngster for only 10 days, then take it away so they may go to nest again. This is how you set certain pairs up for certain races. For instance, if a particular hen flys best at 14 days on eggs, you must take away her eggs or small youngster 24 days before that race. This allows for her 10-day laying cycle plus the 14 days till the race. Checking the

"Motta," from the same loft as "Young Patrick," is another old-bird flyer kept in prime condition.

NEST - 15 - FLYERS - PAIR - II   NEST -15- FLYERS- PAIR II

AU-67-B-576   AU-67- LC- 2145   576 - NOTES - 2145
DARK- CH- COCK   SMOKEY- BL.CH HEN

Color	Band No.	Laid	Clip	Hatch	Notes
SM. BL.CH. *Sire mate*	AU-69-B-711	2/27	on 3 time	on 3/18	Mated up with no problems
SM. BL.CH.	AU-69-B-712				Laid 8 days after mating.
					Both very good on nest.
Moved 711 to nest 6					576 Likes to carry straw from outside.
SM. BL. CH. WFCT -736		4/6 4/8	on time	4/24	On Driving to nest 576 Does not drive hard and doesnot run himself on 2145 out of condition.
SM. BL.Ch. SPL -737					
736 and 737 moved to nest 6					858 from nest 12 tried to fence 576 out of his nest one of his youngsters
Lost 2145 on the 300 mile out for 2 wks. she returned Hurt. cut chest-keel and foot. also has some wing. Put 2145 over with young birds. Mated 576 with 840					* 711 got cut on the back. 576's right eye swelled shut.
736 } gave to Mr. T. Bocek 737 }					lost 2145 on 300 mile ypcc

A typical page from E. C. Welty's record-book, flyers' section. (See also page 192.)

128

breeding records will tell if this hen lays sooner or later than the 10-day laying cycle.

Some of the best champions in the world fly their pigeons by setting particular pairs up for certain races. They do not rely on luck, but on their skill and complete flying and breeding records.

One fancier in particular has a cock that won four races in four consecutive years, all at the same distance and the same nest position [status of the eggs or of the young]. This smart fancier knew that having a 14-day-old youngster in the nest made this pigeon fly his best at this particular race-station. In checking your

Although a hen, this stock-bird has a massive head and gives the impression of great strength. She has proved to be an excellent breeder.

flying records you will be surprised to find that this is true with the greater percentage of the old birds. But most fanciers fail to realize this and fly year after year by guess-work.

It is best to have four van-tosses before the first race. This not only adjusts the old racers into breaking from the flock, but it also gives you an idea on what birds are training best. Do not change from last year's patterns, but try always to have somebody there to drive them in with the aid of the loft stick.

The coopie must also be used as often as possible in these training-tosses. Just like the racers, the coopie must also be retrained to renew what he learned last year.

Feeding Old-Bird Flyers

As with young birds, the golden rule is "Never overfeed your pigeons." If a top-quality feed is given, kept to a regulated daily amount, and adjusted when you feel adjusting is necessary, the birds will fly well. As with young birds, old flyers' daily feedings should vary with weather and race conditions.

It is wise to consider your pigeons athletes and treat them as such. They are athletes of speed, and any extra weight is sure to slow them up. Even in football the trainers know that all extra weight must be taken off the players and that their muscles must be developed. In fact, extensive weight-lifting schedules are set by all football clubs, and any overweight is handled by fining the players. When the birds are overweight you are only fining yourself by being low in the race standards.

When purchasing feed, try to buy enough to last the entire season. The pigeons' digestive systems can easily be upset by a change in feed, and this always throws them out of condition. The only reason feed should be changed is if the quality is not doing your pigeons the most good,* and then make a very gradual change over a period of time.

---

*We are talking here about good, sound feed that is of questionable benefit. Mouldy or otherwise contaminated feed must be disposed of at once, as directed on page 45. Remember, too, that instructions for keeping your pigeons' feed free of contamination, even while it is in storage, were given on page 45. And you can build such storage facilities yourself.

Many fanciers raise only one youngster per nest, so that squabs can be moved from the flyers to the breeders. Here, SC 65 HPC 698 (a Huysken Van Riel cross, blue-check). Although never flown, this cock has sired six winners and is the grand-sire of 11 more.

Condition

What is racing condition and how do you know when your birds are in condition? Each fancier looks for certain things that he feels are signs of condition. They vary greatly, and to list all of them would only confuse you.

The pigeon's general appearance should be bright-eyed, with the feathers showing much color and brightness. The bird should be very alert and constantly moving about cooing, fighting, and looking for trouble with other birds. They should always be anxious to leave the loft for exercise and show much pep while in the air. When landing they should show no stress—and the males upon landing should coo, strut about, and chase the hens. If left outside, they will often leave the loft with a loud banging of the wings and show pleasure in flying. If you find that the birds are tired and listless, you will have to do a lot of work to bring them into condition.

When you pick your pigeons up, the feathers must feel soft and silky. The body should have no excess weight and should feel "corky" or like a tennis ball. The pigeon's eyes should be bright and shiny, with a certain sparkle. The eyes should be alert, and the pupils must be able to dilate quickly whenever the light changes.

Turn the bird over and spread the feathers that cover the breast-bone: the skin should be pink with an absence of scale. A pigeon with scale is not in condition, and you will have to do much work to bring him into form. There may also be a very small bubble of blood formed on the breast-bone. This is a sign of top condition, but it does not always show in every pigeon. If the bubble has turned into a small red streak, then there is a good chance that the bird is going out of condition. The vents should be tight and firm and should lay up into the body.

Your bird's feet should be warm, and pigeon droppings should not adhere to the bottoms. In fact, the feet should give the impression that they were just washed. The legs and toes should also be void of dried scale.

Pigeons in good racing condition are always anxious to eat, but never fill up their crops. In fact, it is a natural process for feed intake to decline when the pigeon is in racing condition. A pigeon in condition will generally eat approximately one half of its normal intake during non-racing times of the year, and no ill effects are ever shown. This proves that it is not necessary to feed heavy to keep your pigeons healthy.

The pigeon's throat must be pink, with no excess mucus. The opening of the windpipe must lie down against the back of the tongue when the mouth is open for inspection. If the pigeon's windpipe opens and closes with a slight protrusion forwards, you know that he is having difficulty in breathing and that his respiratory system is not in condition. The opening of the windpipe is one of the most important parts of the respiratory system. It is situated at the back of the mouth at the end of the tongue and should be small, oval, and rather narrow. The edge round the opening should be fine without any inflammation of the mucous membranes. The windpipe should never make the slightest movement during the pigeon's respiration. The tongue should lie flat in the lower part of the mouth without any movement.

The esophagus is where the food passes. It is very wide and should be free of inflammation and excess mucus.

The tonsil is found at the back of the mouth just above the opening of the esophagus. The lower edge of the tonsil should be notched, giving the impression of small teeth. If the "teeth" are missing, the pigeon had throat canker at one time in its life. The tonsil should be pink without any marks or spots and should lie against the back of the throat.

The best way to open your pigeon's beak is to put your thumb on the lower point of the beak and push the head gently backward. This makes the back of the pigeon's head lie against his back. If you handle him very gently, he will open his beak very easily and enable you to examine the throat.

The mouth should always be clear, without mucus, and should be pink and clean.

One of the most reliable sources in determining condition is the pigeon's droppings. They should be small, firm, tipped with white and have a few down feathers mixed with them. After a night's rest the pigeon's droppings should be piled all in one spot. This shows that nothing is disturbing the pigeon and that he is resting well at night. If the droppings are scattered about, you can be sure that something is bothering the bird. The digestive system may be upset; he may be scratching because of insects; or some animal may be bothering him by prowling round the loft at night.

The color of the droppings depends on the diet. A pigeon that is out a lot or gets a lot of greens has droppings that are dark green in color. Green droppings when a pigeon is on a green-free diet are very undesirable and indicate digestive inflammation or worms.

NOTE: Greens should be kept in the normal diet, but if the droppings become watery when the birds are in the racing season, omit the greens. Watery droppings will put a race bird out of condition.

Pigeons whose diets are low in legumes (peas and beans) and

rich in cereal grains such as corn, wheat, and the like, have very pale droppings. The only time you should be worried about the color is if it varies greatly from what the diet dictates. A change in color is the first sign of digestive problems, and the pigeon droppings should be checked daily.

Pigeons that drink a lot as a result of hot weather, exercise, training-tosses, or a race will quickly develop watery droppings. This is normal for a pigeon that has been deprived of water. When a *rested* pigeon has an abnormal thirst, it is a sign of digestive trouble, which, if ignored, leads to only mediocre condition.

Whatever the reason, no watery droppings should be left unchecked: some preventative and/or remedial measure should be taken or you will never get your birds in top condition.

Choosing old birds, like these, for the races should involve very little guess-work, as your record-book will tell you which birds fly best at various nest positions.

Picking Old Birds for the Race

You should use very little guess-work in picking old birds for the races. Choose certain birds, ahead of time, for particular races and condition them accordingly. Remember, too, that *certain birds fly better at different nest positions*. This kind of selecting allows you to concentrate on certain birds and it makes conditioning much easier as compared with your trying to bring a whole flock into condition. (Contrast these tactics with the hints on picking your entries for the young-bird races—on page 114.)

The process of setting up certain birds for particular races also gives you the advantage of having to transport fewer birds. Thus you cut down considerably on the cost and also increase your chances of placing high on the pool sheets. As with young birds, the old birds that are training the best and are coming first off the training van should be the ones you pick for the top pools.

The trapping and clocking of old birds are identical to what you do with young birds. The only exception is that the old birds have a tendency to land quicker and very often are not seen before they have landed. Remember that young birds fly home for their perch and feed, but old birds have a greater desire for homing to their nest, mate, eggs, or young.

Tricks of the Trade

If the fancier is smart he will be able to get more out of his birds by playing little tricks on them to help increase their homing desire.

During the night place an intruder in the nest and try to place him between the hen and her mate. In the morning the male will find him and drive him away with jealous rage. Put the same bird in the nest regularly until a strong hate develops between the two. This often works very successfully with old birds.

Placing an egg that is just chipping under a bird a few hours before it is to be transported to the race often helps that bird's speed in homing.

On Thursday, remove the nest bowl and close the nest, forcing the pair to perch elsewhere and creating much excitement and anxiety. One hour before you ship to the race, open the nest box and give them back their nest bowl. Their joy and appreciation is demonstrated by their often being first in the clock.

These are just three of the many tricks that you may play on your pigeons to induce them to home faster. Be careful to use these tricks only on the short races though. To send an excited pigeon to a long race is flirting with disaster. They are so excited to be released and to reach home that upon liberation they fly their hearts out, and if the distance is too great, they soon run out of strength and fall far behind.

Long-Distance Racing

It is an established fact that there are certain families or strains that do not win at the short distances, but excel in the hard, difficult long-distance races. These strains come from the lofts of fanciers who specialize in long-distance racing and through years of selective breeding have produced a strain of long-distance winners.

Another long-distance champion, "Barcelona" has placed 20th in international European races.

"Prince," a long-distance flyer, came in 69th in the Barcelona International race held in 1970.

Any strain that gives you pigeons that are able to fly the short, medium, and long races with equal success is rare. And in most cases it is usually an individual bird instead of a particular strain.

Most of the long-distance champions know that young birds must not be raced hard, but that they should be trained well and shipped to only one or possibly two short races and then rested for the winter. It is an exception when a young bird is flown hard and in the following years becomes a long-distance champion. Remember, it is a must to make every effort to allow the pigeon to attain his full physical and psychological development without hindrance if you want to develop a long-distance champion.

Fly your yearlings moderately and send them only to races no greater than 400 miles. An argument could arise from this last statement because there are many long-distance races (500- and 600-miles) that are won by yearlings. This fact cannot be changed, but the point is that to win long-distance races repeatedly, you must develop a team of reliable old birds. Too often these long-distance yearling–winners are placed back in another

137

long race and never return. This would lead one to believe that the yearling's victory may have had a little luck to it instead of a champion performance. To be a long-distance champion you cannot rely on luck, but only on skill and patience to develop a long-distance family.

Pigeons that are to be used in the long-distances should not be flown hard previously. They may fly up to the 300-mile race, but even this flying must be done no later than two weeks before the big race.

Most long-distance champions have found that pigeons between 3 and 6 years of age make the best long-distance flyers, but only if they were not flown hard previous to 3 years of age.

In Belgium any fancier who excels at racing, either short or long, is called a master. This master has become one because he was a manager, teacher, an excellent breeder, and a man of great patience. Are you going to be a master or are you going to settle for being a luck-flyer?

The biggest reason why fanciers are unable to master long-distance races is because they become too anxious to win and, being unable to do so, settle for competing in the shorter races. Remember in becoming a master: it will take years of hard work and *patience* to succeed, and any lesser effort will bring only moderate success or even complete failure.

The best stock to pick for future long-distance races are the descendants of birds with great longevity, whose vitality and power are in evidence up till their older years.

Preparing for Long-Distance Races

Only pigeons that are in an excellent state of health and condition should be considered when you pick your contestants for the long races. Pigeons of top condition use as little energy as possible when flying, and this restraint enables them to stay on the wing for long periods of time. These birds are not the short-distance sprinters, but are considered pluggers that are able to fly continuously without any apparent stress. This is why the long-distance pigeon should be kept calm and sent to the race with the correct mental attitude. This is best obtained by having

Longevity and a muscular build are essential for long-distance success. Tarzan has been winning prizes in the St. Sebastian International races since 1953.

them down on eggs or with a youngster eight days old. Whatever the nest position, make sure that your flyers are not in the milk stage because with the extended period the birds must spend in the transportation crates, this milk may sour the crop. For some unknown reason hens have a tendency to fly better to eggs while cocks fly better to a youngster.

Do not neglect hens when choosing for long-distance races. It has been found that hens fly just as well, if not better, than cocks and win many races at 500 and 600 miles. The only precaution you must take with hens is to be sure that they are not sent to races just after laying. They should be sitting at least 8 days on their eggs. These 8 days allow time for rest and for the hen's system to return to normal. The best nest position for long races—with both hens and cocks—is between 10 and 14 days. Probably more races are won at this nest position than at any other time.

The long-distance flyer must be handled completely differently from the short-distance speed racer. He must not be fed the same and he must be kept calm, not like the nervous short-distance speedster. Nervous pigeons lose their top condition when crated for a couple of days; this is not true of the calm pigeon.

Many fanciers add larger grains, such as corn and peas, to the feed-mixture when the long-distance races approach. In return they lessen the quantity of smaller grains such as wheat and rice, and almost completely remove exciting seeds such as linseed, hemp, and rape seed. This increase in carbohydrates and proteins helps strengthen the muscles and builds up reserve energy. A pigeon winning a long-distance race is like the cross-country runner who knows that, to win, he must be careful to save enough energy for the final miles of the race. This is where top condition plus proper mental attitude wins over anything of lesser quality.

It has been found that most of the long-distance flyers are medium or small in build, with plenty of muscle and a large, sufficient wing-span. Heavier birds are handicapped when their wings are not in correct proportion to the rest of their bodies. The wings must be supple enough to hold the pigeon in flight for long periods of time.

You will find that the long-distance master is admired by all and that there is a much bigger demand for his birds than for those of the short-distance ace. Although both are just as good pigeon-men, the champion long-distance flyer is scarcer. And this creates a much bigger demand for his birds.

No matter what distance you choose to make your specialty, each takes much work and patience. Do not get discouraged at your failures, but treat them as lessons and learn from your mistakes. Every time you win or lose, ask yourself ''What was the reason?'' and ''What can I do next week to improve myself?'' This is the only way you will learn. Do not make the same mistakes week after week, however: teach yourself to recognize mistakes.

After the Long-Distance Race

After the race you should make every effort to allow your long-distance flyers complete rest. It is advisable to feed them only small grains for a few days to allow their digestive systems to return to normal.

Following are some of the tonics you can put into their drinking water to help restore the flyers' lost energy.*

1. Three tablespoons of sugar plus 1 tablespoon of glucose mixed with 2 pints of hot water. Add this mixture to a quart of fresh water. Serve *lukewarm*. When your pigeons arrive back from a race, you should not give them cold water for the remainder of that day.

2. A teaspoon of honey added to hot water and served lukewarm.

3. Effervescent salts in water. This settles the birds' digestive systems and gives them a mild physic.

4. One ounce of tincture of gentian and 1 ounce of tincture of iron mixed with 4 ounces of honey. Use 1 tablespoon of this mixture to 1 gallon of water.

5. A compound syrup of hypophosphites: use 1 tablespoon to a gallon of water.

6. Cod liver oil—either in capsule form or added to their feed.

7. Two teaspoons of syrup of rhubarb mixed with hot water and added to 2 quarts of fresh drinking water. This tonic is often used as a blood purifier.

8. One teaspoon of baking soda added to tepid drinking water.

These are just a few of the many hundreds of tonics that have been used to restore lost energy, and they should be used sparingly. Do not feel that they will bring success and win races for you because nothing can be given that will enable the pigeon

*In the formulas advised throughout this book, 1 pint equals 16 ounces, and the quart is the U.S. quart.

to fly faster and win races. If it were this easy, then the sport of pigeon racing would have vanished years ago. Winning can come only through proper care. It is this that enables your pigeons to maintain health and stamina.

The day after a race, give your flyers a lukewarm bath to relax the muscles. This also gives them a feeling of security.

Much caution should be taken in returning your long-distance flyer to the training schedule. Guide yourself by the distance the bird has flown and how hard the race was.

If a bird has placed well in the long race, most fanciers will be content with its performance and will not fly it any more that season. This allows it to go through a better moult and assures you of its services for next year's race season. On the other hand, some fanciers will not be satisfied in placing high. They will ship their winning long-distancer off to another race before the bird is back in condition—and to their disappointment, wonder why it never comes back home. These fanciers deserve to lose their champions because they are unable to recognize that pigeons are living creatures and are therefore unable to perform like a machine. Do not be afraid to rest pigeons of value because there is always next year.

14. WINNING SYSTEMS

The biggest reason for the popularity of the sport of pigeon racing is that so many different ideas and theories can be used to achieve the same goal. Although there are certain rules that must be abided by, their variations are so great that every fancier may use his own interpretation and call it his system. Not only is there a great love for the birds involved, but competition and variety add spice to this wonderful sport.

This chapter will reveal some different winning systems that are used by successful Pittsburgh fanciers. Although these systems are basically the same and each fancier is trying to arrive at the same results, you will see that there are great variations that make each a separate system. This important chapter will synthesize many ideas that have been discussed in this book. Read it carefully, and it will answer many of your questions.

All the fanciers involved were personally interviewed, and each one was more than glad to tell of his winning system. These are their own personal theories, and the following is what works for each of them.

Raymond (Whitey) Dinkfelt

Whitey, as he is known to his friends, started with fancy pigeons when he was 8 years old. In 1955 he parted with his fancy birds and made room for some racing pigeons. In 1957 he

This entire structure is champion Dinkfelt's loft. Free bobbing is an important part of his birds' exercise schedule.

started flying and has been flying a consistent pigeon ever since. His best birds come down from three pigeons: (1) his good grizzle cock from the Keiper loft, (2) 567 a Huysken Van Riel cock, and (3) Number 1,000, Huysken Van Riel hen. Both his Huysken Van Riels were purchased through Dr. Whitney. Number 567 is a full brother to the famous Three Thousand Dollar cock that is descended from Dr. Whitney's famous 531 blue-checkered cock. Most of his birds are splashes and checkers, and Whitey openly admits that the splashes fly rings round the

The foundation cock of the Raymond Dinkfelt loft: No. 567, a Huysken Van Riel, flies the natural system.

Here, Dinkfelt's famous Huysken Van Riel hen (left) and her mate. Dinkfelt has built up a championship loft, using the inbreeding technique.

checkers. As you can see, his best birds and most of his champions are bred round only three pigeons and their offspring.

Feeding is the key to health and success, Whitey maintains— and because of this belief, he mixes his own feed, using nothing but the best grains available. For three days after a race the birds get nothing but wheat, corn, barley, and rice. The other four days he feeds them his regular mixture. Whitey does not believe in small seeds like linseed and rape and hemp seed (especially hemp seeds). When he fed hemp seed he had a great deal of trouble with flight feathers breaking. When hemp was discontinued all the trouble ceased. In place of these small seeds, he feeds heavier on the wheat.

Every Sunday after the race he puts Sulmet* in the birds' drinking water; on Mondays he puts in a mild solution of piperazine† ; and the rest of the week he adds Vitamin B-1. Fresh grit is given daily. Whitey never feeds greens and he does not believe in giving birds a laxative.

He feels that heavy training is not necessary. Free bobbing (open-loft) plus four 20-mile tosses a week is plenty to get the birds in condition. With this modified training schedule, he has to keep a strict feeding program to help keep the birds' weight down.

Whitey uses a lime and sand mixture on the floor and cleans the loft twice daily (365 days a year).

He gives the flyers a bath every Thursday and the day after every race, but the breeders have bath water in front of them every day.

One thing that he will not do is cure a sick pigeon. Once a pigeon becomes sick, it is immediately destroyed because he feels that a sick pigeon never fully recovers.

Whitey states that he owes all of his success to his wife Bernice. She is more than capable of handling all the loft chores, and this helps tremendously in keeping his pigeons in excellent health.

---

*Sulmet is also known by the longer name, sulphamethazine.
†piperazine is a worm-killer.

Stanley E. Dworek

Stan started with pigeons 21 years ago when his boys brought home some common street-pigeons. Even then he knew the importance of quality stock, so the commons were re-placed with racing pigeons. He received some Stassarts from Mike Kollar and some Stassart-Sion crosses from Ed Finnegan, and for 21 years this family of pigeons has been maintained and flown with much success. He also added some Huysken Van Riels to his loft. He places equally well in the long and short races, and for these, the birds are divided into two different teams.

Stan gives six reasons for his success and he says that, although there are many tricks to the trade, you still must have only a few basic rules to go by and never change them.

1. Fresh, clean water with the addition of Myzon twice a week.

2. Fresh grit daily and a good, sound feed-mixture.

3. Watch the amount of feed given and never allow the birds to get fat.

4. Keeping the birds tough by hard training, flagging them when needed, and free bobbing.

5. Another must is that after every race the birds are fed only a light grain.

6. The most important item is never to crowd your pigeons. Stan readily admits that he used to keep many pigeons and says it was not until he cut down on the flock that he arrived at his success.

Stan's system must truly work because he has won many Average Speeds, a Hall of Fame, three All-American Awards, and—in the past 12 years—three Grand Championships. This is truly a mark of a champion.

Emil Kostkas

Emil believes that the only way to be consistently successful is to build a good family of pigeons and not to keep changing one's stock. Most of his birds are of the Huysken Van Riel strain, and he feels that Van Riels are very good on the nest, very calm and, moreover, have excessive desire and determination.

The birds are fed a good, sound commercial feed-mixture, and he gives them a little rice and linseed as a treat. He carefully controls the amount of feed so that his birds do not develop excess fat.

He is strictly against any medication in the water because he feels that there are no fancy secrets and methods: "just good care 365 days of the year." About the only thing he adds to the water is a little honey after a hard fly. Also, a touch of iodine (10 drops per gallon of water) is put in the birds' water twice a week to kill bacteria in the birds' systems and aid in the hatching of young. Fresh grit is given daily. The birds are given a bath once a week—twice if possible—but never after Wednesday. Emil uses Stay-dri litter on the floor, and since he started using it, there has been less sickness among his birds and the loft stays drier.

As for training, the short tosses seem to work best. Emil's birds receive as many short tosses as possible, with two 60-mile van-tosses weekly. These tosses plus normal exercise about the loft suffice to put the birds in top condition. Emil also lists six items that he feels are most important in spotting condition and becoming a champion.

1. The most reliable source is the droppings. They should be small, firm, tipped with white, and have a few down feathers mixed with them.

2. The two worst enemies in keeping pigeons are overcrowding and overfeeding.

3. The pigeon's eyes should always be bright with small, alert pupils.

4. The legs and breast should be clean without scale.

5. The feathers should always be bright and shiny.

6. The most important item in keeping and flying a good pigeon is to treat it with love and care. This ensures the pigeon's love of the loft and always brings it home faster.

Lou Arcuri

Lou Arcuri is one of the better long-distance flyers in the Pittsburgh area. His wins are numerous, especially at 500 and 600 miles.

About the only family of birds which Lou keeps are some Trentons that come down from Silverchiefs and Eli Morton. The rest of his team are many strains that come from just as many good lofts. He does not care what the strain is just so the pigeons do their job.

Lou raises two teams of young birds each year: one team for club races and the other for open races. His old-bird team consists of 40 birds, and he also keeps 20 pairs of breeders. The reason so many breeders are kept is that he is very strict when it comes to culling weak pigeons. He has no mercy on them, and they just do not stay.

He feeds a regular commercial feed-mixture; but as the distance the birds fly increases, he adds corn and peas. Fresh grit is added daily, and the water is always clean and fresh. He adds nothing to the water except a vitamin powder once a week. He does not believe in medication of any kind, but admits that he *has* tried almost everything there is to try in the water. After years of experimenting, the only conclusion he has drawn is that if the birds are healthy, they do not need anything extra in their water.

Lou's birds are flock-tossed with plenty of short tosses and are shipped twice a week on the training van. They are flagged 45 minutes in the morning and 45 minutes in the evening. This system of handling the birds has been very successful for Lou. By his being tough with the birds, they in return show that they are tough by coming through on race-day whether it is a short or long race.

Lou gives all his birds a bath every Monday. Sand is kept on the floor and it is raked once a week. The loft is kept full of plenty of fresh air and sunlight at all times.

Summary of Winning Systems

The fanciers whose systems are described in this chapter could not give their entire methods because of limited space, but each gave his personal feelings of what is most important. The reason these four were chosen is that they all fly a good pigeon and are considered to be pigeon-flyers of the same calibre.

As you have read, these four fanciers may agree on certain subjects such as grit and good-quality feed, but they differ completely in their views on training, medication, and strains. The importance of this chapter is in showing you that many different ideas and theories may be put together to end up with the same result: a champion pigeon-flyer.

15. WIDOWHOOD SYSTEM

The natural system* (wherein hens and cocks fly to nest) is only one of the systems used in pigeon racing. Other systems such as widowhood and semi-widowhood are very popular, especially in Belgium and other European countries. In the United States, the widowhood system is second in popularity only to the natural system. However, some clubs have outlawed the widowhood system because those fanciers who fly their pigeons on the widowhood system win most of the pools—and it is believed that they win more than their share of races over the non-widowhood-flyers!

Before we continue, it should be made clear that widowhood is one of the most complicated systems and that there are so many variations of this system as to have filled many books. All this chapter intends to do is give you a general idea on widowhood: any variations are left to your own discrimination.

Semi-widowhood is not so popular as full widowhood. The latter gives remarkable results, but as its name implies, it uses only the cocks. The really big drawback with this system is that

*That is, the hens and cocks are permitted to brood their eggs and sometimes hatch a youngster or youngsters.

"The Young Ijzeren," another famous Barcelona International winner, is also flown on the widowhood system.

many good hens are wasted by not being flown. If you look at the results in the natural system you will probably find that just as many hens win races as do cocks.

The biggest advantage in widowhood is that fewer birds have to be kept. For in the natural system where the pigeons are flying to nest, the racers will stay in condition for shorter periods and their peak form will last only 1 or 2 weeks—then they must be brought back into condition, and this may take weeks. A widowhood pigeon can be brought into form early and it will stay in form for at least 8 weeks. This enables the widowhood cock to be sent again and again to the races, but with the natural system birds must be rested and also kept home for many other reasons such as laying and driving to nest. A good pigeon fancier who owns 10 widowers or less, will be far superior at racing success than the fancier who has 30 or 40 birds that are on the natural system.

The widowhood system is especially popular in Belgium. "Bonten," from a Belgian loft, is a prize widower flyer that has scored success in the Barcelona Internationals.

The Widowhood Loft

The widowhood loft should have large windows hinged so that they open wide to allow the race bird to enter. There should be no landing board and no stall trap, but just the open window through which the widower flies directly into his nest box. There he is clocked.

The nest box should have double compartments with the hen being confined on one side until the widower is clocked. The widowhood nest box must be larger than the nest box used in the natural system, for this nest box is the widower–racer's constant home. Moreover, when he arrives back from the race he flies through the window directly to the nest box. Therefore it must be big enough for him to land easily within it.

Construct all windows and entrances to close. You should also be able to attach some type of shades or shutters to them to

This widowhood loft has been built above a one-storey garage. Note the large windows that enable the widowers to fly through, directly to their nests.

darken the loft. The reason for this is so that the widower pigeons are unable to see other pigeons flying about. Also, the darkness keeps them in a state of rest and relaxation. The big principle in the widowhood system is to keep the birds as calm as possible during the week. Only on the day before being sent off to a race should the cock be excited by the showing of his hen.

In summing up the widowhood loft it can be said that it is built much the same as the natural-system loft (page 16) except that it has larger windows, larger nest boxes and can be darkened. Besides these three points, it lacks a landing board and has no perches and no stall traps.

Mating Widowers

Some fanciers mate their widowers prior to the race season and let them raise one youngster to a nest. When the youngster is weaned, the hen is then removed and the cock goes into the widowhood system.

Other fanciers only allow their future widowers to go to eggs, and the eggs are removed at 12 days. Then, at the end of the race season the widowers are permitted to raise a youngster.

Some fanciers do not even mate their widowers before the race season, but put them directly on widowhood. After the races they are permitted to mate and to raise a youngster.

Many widowhood fanciers allow their birds to fly the first race on the natural system, and upon their return, the mate and one egg are removed. On the second day, the second egg and the nest bowl are removed. This last act officially puts the birds on the widowhood system. As you can see, the variations in this system are countless.

Training Widowers

It is best to start your future widower birds on their roadwork while they are still mated. This improves their homing instinct and sharpens their senses. Since the widowers do not need much roadwork, any training they get previous to going on widowhood can be nothing but beneficial to them.

After being put on widowhood the cocks may or may not be trained previous to 10 days before the first race, as just 10 days is sufficient to train widowhood cocks. The widowers must then be given at least three 25-mile tosses before the first race. Most fanciers do not show the widowers their mates when the birds return from their training flights.

Forced Flying

In all sports, training is essential to keep the athlete in good condition, and this is also true with widowers. Although they do not need much roadwork to sharpen their homing instincts, they still need plenty of exercise to keep their muscles and respiratory system in top working order. Forced flying (flagging) has been found to be absolutely essential for widowers.

Forced flying must be started slowly and should be increased a little each day until your birds reach the desired time they must spend exercising. Twice a day, lock the widowers out of the nest and force them to fly their allotted time. Do not let them do any free bobbing, but strictly regulate all their training flights and all their flagged flying.

Once the widowhood system is in effect you must run everything on a strict timetable and make sure that every event of the day is done precisely on time. The forced flights, feeding, and everything else should be a daily routine. Any variation will only upset the widowers. Keep constantly in mind that *the only thing you want your birds to be concerned about is their mates and their nests.* Anything else may excite them and make them useless as widowers.

Feeding the Widower

Feeding may also vary when you put your birds on the widowhood system. Some fanciers actually count grains or weigh specific amounts when feeding, and others keep feed in front of the birds at all times. It has been found that no matter how much is fed, a good widower will never become fat. The drawback with feeding large quantities is that great amounts are scattered about and much is wasted.

All feeding and watering is done in the widower's nest box. Each nest box contains separate cups, one for water and one for feed. These cups are attached on the outside so that they are easier to fill. This also prevents any dirt from entering and contaminating the feed and water.

Only grains that are high in protein and carbohydrates should be used in the widowers' regular mixture. Eliminate the small exciting seeds such as rape seed, linseed, and hemp seed from the regular mixture. Feed these only when your widowers return from a race or on the day after a race. These seeds must be introduced into the diet only for the purpose of fast trapping.

Preparing the Widower for the Race

On the day of shipping, the widower must have complete rest and relaxation. The loft must be kept dark, and nobody should enter the loft until the time of shipping.

At the very last minute, put the widowers into the crates, take them only a few miles and release them to fly home. Upon arrival allow the cocks to see their hens, but they must not be allowed to tread. After they see their mates, place the widowers in the special widowhood crate and take them to the club for shipping.

If the birds were fed in the morning you will find it unnecessary to feed them in the afternoon. The training and their seeing of their hens take their minds off food and put them in a state of excitement so great that upon release every bird's only thought is to hurry home to its waiting mate.

The Widowhood Hens

You must take great care in choosing the hens to be used in the widowhood system. They must be very affectionate and must also show much love for their mates.

Widowhood hens must be affectionate by nature and very demonstrative toward their mates—otherwise the system will not work. This hen, from Belgium, has proved an ideal "widower's" mate. She is the sister of the famous Coffi Coethryssee.

Upon return of the widower, the hen must greet him with love and affection and must show great excitement. A hen that is not rank or ardent is very discouraging to the widowhood cock and sometimes may ruin him for this type of flying.

Your first job after sending the widowers off is to prepare the hens so that they show much love to their returning mates. Two days prior to the race, the hen should be fed the exciting seeds (rape, hemp, and linseed). This helps prepare her for the return of her mate. On shipping night, allow the hens out to fly. Lock them out for at least 45 minutes. This helps them physically and excites them for the want of their nests. At the end of the 45 minutes, open the window to allow them to fly into their nests. Then lock them in.

On the morning of the race, feed the hen plenty of big grains so she will not want the small grains that are presented to the widower upon his return. Also, this will prevent her from wanting to eat when the cocks are fed, but she will instead show plenty of excitement while the widower is eating the small grains.

Before the widowers' arrival home, the nest bowls must be put into the nests. This not only excites the hens, but also adds excitement to the returning widowers.

Before arrival, open the window completely so that there is nothing to obstruct the widower from flying straight into his nest box. Since the hens are confined in a compartment in each nest box you do not have to worry about their leaving the loft.

As soon as the bird has been clocked, allow him to enter the same compartment as the hen and then leave them alone. There is no set rule on how long to leave them together. Most fanciers arrive at this mostly by the distance flown. With a short race of 100 miles the birds may be left together for a few hours, and as the distance increases so does the length of time that they are allowed together.

You must keep the widowhood hens away from the widowers by housing them where the cocks are unable to see or hear them. If a widower discovers where the hens are kept, he will immediately fly to this spot and most likely will become useless as a widowhood flyer. He will lose interest in his nest because he has

These widowhood hens are kept in a section of the loft that is out of sight and hearing distance from the widowers.

been conditioned to associate the hen with the nest: if he knows where she is ordinarily housed he immediately associates her with a location different from his nest. Therefore take great efforts at concealment when you are constructing a place to house the hens.

The Widower's Week

Let us examine a typical week following the widowhood system.

Sunday

Sunday is usually the day of the race. Some countries or areas fly on Saturdays. If this is the case in your locality, move the directions pertaining to each day back one.

When the bird arrives home from the race on Sunday, he must be greeted with calmness. Do not frighten or injure him when catching him for clocking. The clock must be placed in a central location so that it is easily accessible. Some fanciers have a sling made so that they are able to carry the clock over one of their shoulders. This saves precious seconds when clocking.

After the widower and his mate have been together their allotted time, take the hen away with great caution so the cock does not know that you are the one who removed her. The best way to separate them is to show the cock some hemp seed with your left hand, and while he is eating, remove the hen quickly with the right hand. Turn your back toward the nest box and use your body to hide her; then take her away. The cock should not associate you with taking her away, but should be led to believe that she left on her own.

After all your birds are home from the race and the hens are removed, darken the loft and do not disturb the widowers for the rest of the day. Darkness and quiet are very beneficial to the fast recovery of a racing widower. At the end of the day, remove the nest bowls.

Monday

Monday must be a day of complete rest, for this enables the nerves, muscles, digestive system and mental attitude of the racer to return to normal. There are no training-tosses, forced flights, or open-loft on Monday as this only prevents the restoring of energy and does nothing but excite the birds.

Some fanciers give their birds some type of medication or physic, but in a well-maintained loft it is believed to be unnecessary. If you think your birds need it, make the medication mild—using bicarbonate of soda or effervescent salts.

The racers should be fed lightly on Monday, and you should give them only the smaller grains. In the afternoon you may feed greens, excluding lettuce which loosens the bowels. Keep the loft dark and enter it only when absolutely necessary. In this way you ensure the birds of complete rest.

Tuesday

On Tuesday, the widowers should have a forced flight of 15 minutes, no longer. The reason is that this is their first flight since the race and they have not had much food since Saturday and they still have a great desire to enter the loft with hopes of finding their mates. Forcing a pigeon to fly at this stage is cruel and may do more harm than good. They may be fed their regular mixture, but only sparingly. Each day's feeding should be increased. It has been found that if widowers are fed sparingly at the beginning of the week, they will have much better appetites towards the week-end—and this helps considerably in keeping weight down and obtaining the correct mental attitude in your pigeon.

Pigeons that are in good form will regain their proper race weight with 6 to 8 good feedings—or three to four days. They should also be exercised Tuesday evening or given a small training toss of about 10 miles. When they return, feed them sparingly again. Between exercising and feeding times, keep the loft dark so the birds can relax. You should do this darkening not only on Tuesday, but the entire week as well.

Wednesday

On Wednesday morning take the widowers out for a training-toss or flag them for their full time. If they are not trained in the morning, you must give them an evening toss.

By Wednesday they will take plenty of food. This is important if you want them in shape by Sunday's race. Not only is the art of feeding important in young birds and when your pigeons are flying on the natural system, but it is also of the greatest importance in widowhood flying. The widowers must be fed enough, but in such a way that they do not feel that they have had enough.

Give your birds a lukewarm bath Wednesday morning after the training-toss and then darken the loft until their evening feeding.

Thursday

Thursday may also begin with a training-toss of about 25 miles. If you are unable to take the birds out in the morning, give them an early evening toss. They must also have at least one forced flight on Thursday—either in the morning or evening, depending on when they were taken for the training-toss.

On Thursday the widowers must again receive plenty of food. Force them to take only big grains. Do not give any small grains until after they have eaten their fill, and then give only a pinch of hemp or linseed.

Friday

Follow the same routine on Friday with one exception: when the widowers return from their evening flight, you may allow them to see their mates for a few minutes. Do not let them get together, but put the hens in the closed sections of each nest box.

Remove the hens and then feed the widowers. With the excitement of seeing the hens, the widowers' appetites will diminish—thus beginning to prepare them for the race. If your pigeons are in form, there will be much cooing and calling for their mates.

Saturday

On Saturday morning, give your birds their usual exercise, and after the training flight allow them to see their hens for only a few minutes. After the hens are removed, feed the widowers a few dessert seeds as a consolation. Then feed the regular mixture. After they have eaten, darken the loft and do not return until it is time to crate them. As stated before, at the very last minute

A grand-daughter of "Bliksem," this widowhood hen was winning diplomas when she was still too young to be bred. At mating age she bred a winner and is today the grand dam of five winners. A Huysken Van Riel dark-check hen, IF 57 824 is a yellow-eye.

the widowers are put into the crates and are taken a few miles and released to fly home. Upon arrival they are allowed to see their mates, but they must not be allowed to tread.

As an added incentive you may also add the nest bowl when the cocks return from the short training-toss. After taking the cock from the nest bowl, hold him in front of the hen for a few seconds. He must be convinced that the loving hen will be waiting for him upon his return.

Summation of Widowhood

It has often been said that the stimulation brought about by seeing his hen increases the incentive of the racing widower. This stimulation works through the endocrine glands, which also stimulate the pigeon's racing ability. This stimulation may be compared to adrenaline-action on the human being.

Although much more could be said about widowhood flying, a book of this nature, on the general well-being and training of racing pigeons, cannot delve farther into this subject. The widow-hood system offers opportunity for such a wide diversity of methods that it would take hundreds of pages to cover this subject completely. If you find that widowhood is the system of your choice, then purchase one of the books listed on page 205 which are written specifically on the widowhood system. Or see if your local library has them.

To sum up widowhood, it must be said that it is the best system that has ever been devised to bring out the best in the racing pigeon. Although it may have some faults, its good points completely outweigh them. If you have any doubts, then count the number of champions in Belgium who fly the widowhood system as compared with the natural-system champions. Many flyers in the United States were unknown until they adopted the widowhood system.

Remember that although this system brings out the best in a pigeon, it cannot make a good pigeon out of a bad one. If your birds did not perform well under the natural system then they will also fail with widowhood. You must start with good pigeons if you expect to do well.

16. EYE-SIGN

Fanciers use many theories in determining the value of pigeons, and "eye-sign" is probably the most believed of these theories. It has often been said that "The pigeon's eye is his soul." Although the Eye-Sign Theory has never been proven, it is still of great value to the reader because it has such world-wide popularity that there must be at least a kernel of truth to it.

Anybody who has ever kept pigeons has been aware of the keen eyesight that they possess. How many times have you noticed their amazing ability to find small seeds that are mixed in the litter? Or to spot a hawk hundreds of feet in the air when it is almost impossible for you to see it? Pigeons also have the ability to pick their mates out of a flock of pigeons or to spot a home-coming pigeon long before you can.

Pigeons have almost complete all-round vision—called "Monocular Vision." The pigeon's eyes are placed on both sides of the head, which enables them to look forward and backward. There is only a small area directly behind its head that a pigeon cannot see.

A pigeon is unable to take an eye test, but if it were able, we would find that its eyes are far superior to man's.

Eyesight plays an important rôle in the education of pigeons because most of what they learn is through what they see. Eyesight enables a wild pigeon to find food from great heights and it also protects the pigeon by enabling it to spot its enemies in

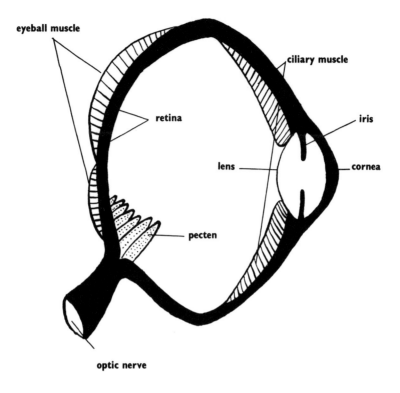

eyeball muscle

ciliary muscle

retina

iris

lens

cornea

pecten

optic nerve

THE EYE

The astuteness of the pigeon's vision has always impressed man. Theory has it that the pecten is responsible for this gift.

time to escape. For the fancier it is an ideal way to determine a pigeon's state of health and condition because eye coloration is one of the first things affected by illness.

The pigeon's eye is basically global with the pupil in the middle. Just behind the pupil is the crystalline lens which is capable of altering the shapes of objects that are focussed on the back of the globe. On the back of the globe (or eyeball) is the light-sensitive retina which has thousands of nerve endings that send the nerve response to the brain. This nerve response is what we call vision. At the back of the eye is a small rod called the "pecten." The exact function of this pecten is not known, but theory has it that it enables the pigeon to see movements and things at great distances. Surrounding the pupil is the iris. The iris contains a circular muscle called the "ciliary" muscle. It is this muscle that enables the pupil to dilate or contract.

The iris should be a deep, solid color that does not look washed out. It is desirable to have an iris of one solid color. An iris with two colors is said to be a "broken eye."

Around the edge of the pupil is a very thin line or outer circle of the pupil. This circle is called the "circle of eye-sign," "the circle of correlation," or the "circle of adaptation."

Some eye-sign specialists have drawn up a Table of Eye-Sign which shows the various shapes and colors of the circle of correlation. They have divided the eye-sign system into a formula of recognition rating from 1 to 10, with Number 1 being no eye-sign and Number 10 being the best. Eye-sign is one of the most complicated and misinterpreted theories in racing pigeons, and to go deep into the subject would be confusing. Following are the ten signs of recognition.

Number One Rating

The bird with the Number-1-rated eye contains no eye-sign at all. If you inspect the bird under a bright light you will find complete absence of any circle surrounding the pupil. Such a pigeon may have an iris of solid color, but because he has no circle to his eye pupil, this pigeon is said to be useless as a long-distance bird.

Number Two Rating

The Number 2 eye-rating is known as "lying sight," and you will find this type of circle lying at the lower half of the pigeon's pupil. It partially encircles the lower 25 per cent of the pupil and is the most common eye-sign. You can compare the appearance of "lying sight" to the moon in its first quarter.

Number Three Rating

The Number-3-rated eye is known as "standing sight." It is similar to the Number 2 eye, only it is located round the upper half of the pupil. This means that if you were to draw a perfectly horizontal line through the pupil, "standing sight" would lie above the line and "lying sight" would be below it.

Number Four Rating

Number 4 or the half circle could be considered the combination of Eye-Signs 2 and 3, in that it runs from the lower half of the pupil to the top. The eye-sign circle may sometimes surround as much as 75 per cent of the pupil.

Number Five Rating

The Number 5 or full circle is a thin line that completely encircles the pupil without any breaks. This eye is often confused with the Number 10, but the difference lies in the width. The Number 5 is only a very fine line and is not nearly so thick as the Number 7 or 10.

Number Six Rating

The Number 6 or serrated (notched) eye is considered to be very good and it could be rated almost as high as the Number 10 eye. The Number 6 is the most uncommon eye to be found. The circle of correlation is solid black and may encircle up to 90 per cent of the pupil. It is very thick, and short rays of black extend from this circle of correlation into the iris. If you have ever seen pictures of the eclipse of the sun, then you may compare the Number 6 sign to this.

Number Seven Rating

The Number 7 or strong circle is exactly what it implies: it is a strong, complete circle that is deep in color. It is usually black, but may also be orange, pearl white, or yellow. There may be other colors, but they are rare.

Number Eight Rating

The Number 8 or "broken sign" is also very rare. It can be considered a bulging Number 2 (lying sight) that can circle up to 90 per cent of the pupil. A pigeon with a Number 8 eye has a very prominent circle-bulge at the lower corner of the pupil — or where lying sight is found. This bulge may extend halfway into the iris.

Number Nine Rating

The Number 9 or Yellow Eye-Sign may be mistaken for a Number 2 at first glance, but if you inspect further, you will find

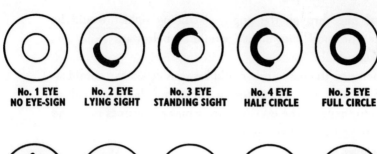

No. 1 EYE NO EYE-SIGN	No. 2 EYE LYING SIGHT	No. 3 EYE STANDING SIGHT	No. 4 EYE HALF CIRCLE	No. 5 EYE FULL CIRCLE

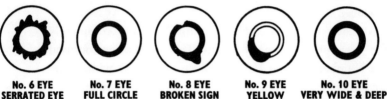

No. 6 EYE SERRATED EYE	No. 7 EYE FULL CIRCLE OR STRONG CIRCLE	No. 8 EYE BROKEN SIGN	No. 9 EYE YELLOW FULL CIRCLE	No. 10 EYE VERY WIDE & DEEP CIRCLE, GREEN OR VIOLET

The 10 different eye-signs are diagrammed in this chart. Eye-sign is one of the data that should be reported in your breeding and flying records to help you determine if the eye-sign is a breeding aid. Note: Vic De Feyter is a fancier who through years of breeding the Havenith strain had much success with them. He used his own breeding program, thus De Feyter's Havenith's came into existence.

a definite full yellow circle that completely engulfs the pupil. You will be able to distinguish the Number 9 eye very easily in pigeons that have solid red eyes. But with pigeons that have a yellow band round the iris, this yellow circle of eye-sign has a tendency to blend in completely, making it difficult for you to detect.

Number Ten Rating

The Number 10 is considered the green or violet eye-sign. It is a wide, solid circle of green or violet which completely encircles the pupil. Number 10 is the most desired eye-sign and is considered the best possible eye that a pigeon may possess.

Thousands of pigeons have been handled, and their eyes have been studied with much interest. It has been found that there is an exception to every rule, and this includes the Eye-Sign Theory. There have been pigeons with Number 10 eyes that were champion breeders and also many that were failures. The Number 25 hen of Ted Bocek was one of his best flyers and without any doubt was the best breeding hen he ever owned. She was void of any eye-sign and had to be rated Number 1 in this formula of recognition.

It has also been noted that certain strains of birds have better eye-sign than others. This could lead you to believe that a fancier having one of these strains, bred by the Eye-Sign Theory, was very successful.

About 1945, the late Julius Boutte of Mishawaka, Indiana, imported a pair of Van Lindens from Belgium. Two youngsters from this pair were sent to the Pittsburgh area and they were responsible for some of the greatest pigeons that ever flew in the Pittsburgh and Mishawaka areas. Many of these pigeons possessed excellent eye-sign, but just as many rated low or were completely without it. No matter what the eye-sign, these birds flew equally well.

No matter what your thoughts are on eye-sign, the only way you can be positive of its value is to mark down in the flying and breeding records what number eye your birds possess. After many years of flying, it may then be possible through experience and record-keeping, to analyze the subject completely and come up with the correct answer.

One point that must be made clear is: No matter what theories you practice, if you win your share, or more, of the races, then what you believe in is correct. If you find winning hard to come by, then read this book again and take steps to improve yourself. It has been found that many fanciers brag about their champion pigeons, but when asked about their victories, you find that they are few and far between. Do not fall into this category, but always be willing to learn by your own mistakes.

17. DISEASES

It is most important that the pigeon fancier be able to spot sickness in the early stages. This chapter will give you some general knowledge about pigeon diseases and parasites so that you can spot the problem before disease destroys a valuable bird or even your entire flock.

The best cure for any disease is prevention. This is accomplished by keeping the birds in the best of health, by starting good habits, and never varying from them. Try to cure sick pigeons at the first sign of sickness, instead of waiting until an epidemic occurs.

Some fanciers believe all sick birds should be killed. This is a complete waste and only shows their ignorance. Although many types of illnesses should be handled by destroying the pigeon, it is not necessary when the illness is no more dangerous than the common cold. This chapter will guide you in disease diagnosis and treatment. Why should a good pigeon be destroyed because its owner did not have the knowledge to treat a minor illness?

Pigeons are most hardy, extremely adaptable and, under good conditions, cause little trouble on grounds of their health. The most important item in maintaining a healthy loft is maintaining proper sanitation and animal husbandry. You should go to great lengths in keeping every inch of your loft spotless.

Sources of Contamination

There is no substitute for good health, and all weaklings should be eliminated from the loft. Do not kid yourself into believing

This is a very dangerous way to keep water: without a proper cover, all dirt and droppings fall into the water, thus contaminating it.

that a weakling will eventually regain his health and become a champion. *This has never happened.* Certain diseases attack pigeons in epidemic proportions. When a disease reaches this scale, its widespread distribution is often the result of ignorance. For instance, a fancier will send an infected bird to the race, thus spreading the disease to other fanciers' race birds (see page 177). These contaminated birds return to their own lofts and drink the water, thus spreading contagion.

Water is the biggest source of contamination. Clean water twice a day, plus cleaning of the waterers, helps to keep down the chance that diseases will spread. Very often an infected rodent or wild bird may drink from the bath or drinking water. This is a very dangerous situation, and you should take great precautions to make your loft pest-free.

Moreover, all wild birds must be kept from even entering the loft because all wild birds carry at least one type of disease that may be transferrable to your pigeons.

Often a sick pigeon will regurgitate his feed, and a healthy bird will pick up the infected grains. This source of contamination is hard to prevent, so the only thing you can do is to *clean up any uneaten grains* and, upon noticing a sick pigeon, isolate him immediately.

The biggest factor in having sickness or epidemics among your birds is *overcrowding the loft.*

Overcrowding the Loft

Many chapters could be written on this subject alone. Because of limited space, however, we are going to condense the subject of overcrowding here. Nevertheless, read this section very carefully, remember it, and you will never go wrong.

1. A major cause of the spreading of disease is overcrowding. This should be sufficient reason for you to keep the amount of birds down to a minimum.

2. Confusion always prevails in a crowded loft. There is much fighting, and the shyer birds are constantly being pushed about. Once a pigeon becomes discontent, he eventually will be lost.

3. More work is connected to a crowded loft. The loft gets dirty twice as fast and during training season it takes twice as many crates and a greater amount of time to catch the birds. When a hobby turns into work, many short-cuts are taken and eventually complete failure befalls you.

4. In a crowded breeding section it is much easier for a hen to be treaded by someone other than her mate. And to maintain a correct breeding plan, it is most important that you are sure of each of your bird's parentage.

5. There is more chance of complaints from people living near

you when large numbers of pigeons are released to fly over their houses.

6. The cost of maintaining a large flock of pigeons is higher than most workingmen can afford. This may lead to family fights, and the quality of grain given may be sacrificed to save on feed bills. Never save by cutting on the quality of feed, but cut down on the amount of birds you keep.

It is impossible to completely eliminate sickness in the loft. Following are the most common diseases to be found in pigeons. To be able to spot sickness and diagnose it correctly will take years of experience, but this will give you a good start!

One-Eye Colds

One-eye colds are probably the most common ailment found in pigeons. A one-eye cold is a bacterial infection that may attack both eyes, but the vast majority of birds will have it in only one eye. It is not the eyeball that becomes infected, but the area round the eyeball. There is a lot of pain, irritation, and watering of the eye.

These symptoms may be the beginning of other diseases, but in one-eye-colds there are no other symptoms. One-eye colds are very simple to treat. Use one of the many eye salves containing antibiotics which are available. One of these is achromycin with 5 per cent hydrocortisone. These antibiotics are very successful in fighting bacterial infections. You can also use boric acid applied with the aid of any eye dropper, or add SQS to the water. Make sure that you set the medicines under each eyelid.

It is essential to isolate the infected bird and disinfect all the waterers in the loft at once. If treated promptly, the infection should clear up within 10 days.

Canker

Canker is a protozoan disease that is the greatest killer and crippler of the pigeon diseases. It has been found that almost every pigeon has canker protozoa (Trichomonas) in the crop, but it is not until the bird's resistance is down that the protozoa can attack the internal organs.

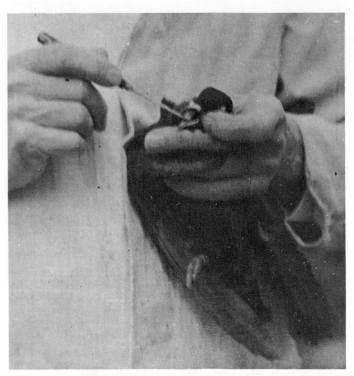

This fancier is removing cheesy canker growths from the mouth of his sick pigeon. When canker strikes, put copper sulphate or aminonitrothiazol in your flock's water for 24 hours, before you do any extractions.

A swelling in the throat and cheesy growths in the mouth are certain signs of canker, but this type is easily treated. A form of canker which attacks young birds is much harder to diagnose and treat, with the navel being the first area to be infected. The navel becomes enlarged with a hard yellow growth and if it is not treated, the protozoa often attack the internal organs.

All forms of canker can be treated if found early. Many different types of medicine are available on the open market for curing canker. Since canker is very common, it is best to be prepared and have one of these medicines on hand in your supply cabinet.

Copper sulphate used at the rate of 35 milligrams to each 100 cubic centimeters of water is very effective in flock-treatment.

Aminonitrothiazol used at the rate of 1,400 milligrams to 4,000 cc of water is another good flock-treatment. Many fanciers have had great success with a commercial product called His-to-seps. This is used as a preventative rather than a cure.

After a day of medication, the cheesy growths in the throat may be gently removed with tweezers. Make sure that there is no excessive bleeding while you are removing the throat canker. If bleeding begins, stop and continue medication, and try again in 24 hours. Canker in the navel is best treated through medication. Some fanciers open the navel and remove the canker, but unless you have some experience it is not advisable. Remember, this form of canker takes much longer to treat.

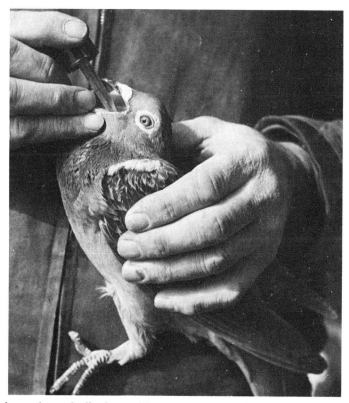

Sour crop is the easiest of all pigeon illnesses to treat. After you have forced the stale water out of the pigeon's crop, use a small syringe to fill the crop again—this time with bicarbonate of soda or some other sweetening agent.

Protection from canker is almost impossible. You must keep your entire flock in the best of health, for this is the only prevention. Once a bird has been exposed though, he is immune for life.

Sour Crop

Sour crop is caused by the bird's eating food that was either unseasoned, wet, sour, mouldy or contaminated in some other way. Filthy drinking water is another source of this trouble. In fact, anything contaminated that enters the crop may lead to sour crop.

In this condition, a great amount of water is drunk by the pigeon because of nausea. There is much vomiting of sour water and grain. If not corrected, sour crop will develop into a more serious condition.

Sour crop is the easiest illness to treat. Hold the bird so that its head is pointed down and very gently, from the bottom of the crop, push upwards, forcing the stale water out of the crop. With a small syringe, fill the crop with some type of sweetening agent. Baking soda, bicarbonate of soda, salt, and crushed charcoal are all effective in sweetening the crop. Do not feed the afflicted pigeon anything for 24 hours, and for five days after this, feed lightly.

Paratyphoid

Paratyphoid, a bacterial disease, may be the most serious disease connected with pigeon-keeping. There have been accounts where it has killed as high as 80 per cent of the loft.

The symptoms in adult pigeons may vary. Swollen joints (usually in the wing), fluid-filled lumps, swelling in the legs, and limping are all signs of paratyphoid. In severe cases, death may occur without any swelling. Diarrhea, ruffled feathers, and drooping wings may also accompany this disease.

If young are dying in the egg and in the nest without any apparent reason, you should suspect paratyphoid. Without much experience, it is hard to be sure of a diagnosis: some birds may form lumps on their wings from a blood clot resulting from an injury. However, if swellings occur in more than one bird, it would be advisable to suspect paratyphoid.

Although there are some medications on the market which cure paratyphoid, experience proves that destroying of the infected pigeon is best and that the medication be used strictly as a preventative.

This disease can be spread by a number of different means, but the highest form of contamination is water and droppings. Flies, wild birds, and rodents are all carriers of paratyphoid. As you read previously, construct your loft so that all forms of vermin are kept out. (The section on discouraging insects, page 185, will help you to eliminate flies from your loft.)

Once you are sure that a bird has contracted paratyphoid, kill or isolate him. Next, treat your entire flock with any of the following medications: tetracyclines, furazolidone, sulphamerazine, or sulphamethazine.

If you are sure that this dreaded disease has infected your pigeons, please *eliminate yourself from race competition and prevent an epidemic.*

Coccidiosis

Coccidiosis, a protozoan disease, is an infection of the intestines that is the principal cause of "going light."* It is another parasite that is present in all pigeons but does no harm until the bird becomes weak through lack of proper loft hygiene.

An infected pigeon becomes droopy, has severe diarrhea, loses much weight and appears anemic. The bird consumes much water with complete loss of appetite, and the diarrhea sometimes becomes so bad that there is bleeding from the rectum.

The only way coccidiosis can be spread is by a pigeon's eating the Coccidia protozoa that have been passed through droppings. Keep your loft completely clean and free of dampness since the Coccidia die upon drying. Make sure that feed is free from droppings.

---

*"Going light" is the term used in connection with a racing pigeon that has lost, or *is* losing, an excessive amount of weight. Going light is not a disease, but a symptom of one.

Any of the drugs used for paratyphoid may be used in treating coccidiosis.

Pox

Pigeon pox, a virus disease, can often disfigure and even kill a pigeon. It is very common in warm climates and usually appears in the fall.

The pox reveals itself in wartlike growths that appear on the unfeathered portions of the bird. There are two forms of pox: the throat pox and the skin-form. The throat pox, or diphtheria, is found only in the throat and has a much higher mortality rate. In the skin-form there are wartlike growths that may become so large that complete areas of the bird's head and legs are covered. Only in rare instances does *skin* pox cause death, and when death does occur, you will most likely find that the pigeon was not healthy in the first place. A healthy pigeon may contract pox, but always to a lesser degree.

The pox virus is carried and transmitted by the mosquito, and the virus can enter only by means of an open sore or wound. Once an infected mosquito bites a pigeon, there is a great chance that pox will appear at the point of puncture. Pox may also be spread through an open wound that was received in fighting with an infected pigeon.

There is no immediate cure for pox: it must run its course. A pigeon-pox vaccine is on the market, and you can use this to vaccinate your birds. But if at all possible, purchase the human vaccine because it is much more effective. It does not hurt to doctor the pox lesions with tincture of iodine, peroxide, mercurochrome, merthiolate or any other medication of this type. In almost all cases there is complete recovery with the skin-form, and upon recovering the pigeon forms complete immunity.

Thrush

Thrush, a fungus infection, is more common in pigeons than most fanciers realize. It occurs mostly in late spring when the

Anyone who is serious about keeping pigeons will have an adequately supplied medicine cabinet in the loft. Malucidin, bicarbonate of soda, piperazine and tetracyclines are a few suggested staples.

rains are the heaviest and, like so many other diseases, it is caused by eating wet, mouldy grains.

Thrush symptoms resemble those of throat canker in that there are yellowish patches in the throat, mouth, and crop. (They are heaviest in the crop.) In the advanced stage there is a slimy discharge that often adheres to the roof of the pigeon's mouth. It also gives the impression of sour crop, but upon examining the empty crop, you will find it much thicker: as if coated with a heavy slime.

These yellow patches may be removed from the throat and mouth with a blunt instrument. Then swab the infected area with tincture of iodine or a boric-acid solution. The antibiotic malucidin is the only known medicine available to treat thrush.

If thrush is present, the entire loft will have to be disinfected. You will also have to disinfect all food and water containers with lye to eliminate any mould or fungi growths.

As explained in almost every chapter, the only preventative is a clean, bright, warm, dry loft.

SPECIAL NOTE: In reading this chapter on diseases it is the authors' hope that you realize that dirt, darkness, and dampness are the three D's leading to disease and disappointment.

The Common Cold

As with human beings, the common cold is just as big a problem for pigeons. There is watering of the eyes, a mucus discharge from the nostrils, and there may be difficulty in breathing and a loss of appetite. If the common cold is allowed to go unchecked, it very often develops into something more serious like roup.

If one of your birds has a cold, treat the entire flock by placing aureomycin, terramycin, or potassium permanganate in their drinking water. It would help to give the infected bird cod liver oil capsules to help raise his resistance.

Swab his infected eyes and nostrils with boric acid or potassium permanganate. Two teaspoons to a pint of water is sufficient.

Roup

Roup or coryza has almost the same symptoms as the common cold, but is much more dangerous. The difference in symptoms is that the mucus discharge from the nostrils may change to a puslike substance, the head may swell and the eyes may shut completely. There may also be sneezing and a rasping cough.

If you are sure that the bird's ailment is roup, it is best to destroy the pigeons because *recovered birds are carriers*. All breezes and dampness should be eliminated from the loft, and thorough sterilization of the loft with lye is necessary. Put some type of medication in the drinking water to prevent the disease from spreading among the surviving birds. Potassium permanganate, sulpha drugs, or penicillin may be used as the preventative.

You have just read about nine of the most common illnesses found in pigeons. So to continue on and describe the less important diseases would only add confusion.

Diseases that attack the digestive system make the pigeon especially weak and unable to perform well in the races.

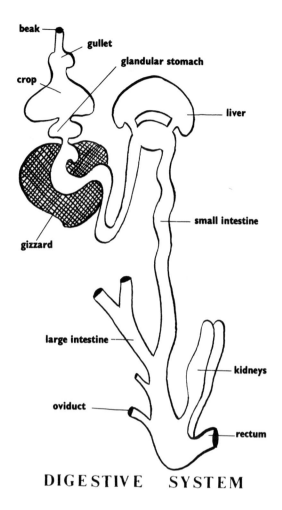

beak
gullet
glandular stomach
crop
liver
gizzard
small intestine
large intestine
kidneys
oviduct
rectum

DIGESTIVE   SYSTEM

A Mystery Illness

In the winter of 1969 the fanciers of the Pittsburgh area were hit with a new type of illness. This illness had the same symptoms as many other pigeon diseases such as coccidiosis and paratyphoid. The difference was that all outer appearances of the birds seemed normal. In fact, if you did not handle your birds you would not know they were sick, but as soon as a bird was picked up, you knew something had to be wrong. They felt as if they were going light with no weight to their bodies, and further observation showed that the droppings were wetter than normal.

181

The pigeons ate, but never enough to fill their crops and they were very weak and had a hard time standing on their legs. The oddest symptom was that only a few birds were sick at one time and, after recovery, within five to seven days different birds became sick.

Droppings from the infected birds were sent to Dr. Whitney. He could not identify the disease, but stated that the bacteria found was often connected with chickens. He suggested that the flocks be treated with terramycin. The terramycin seemed to be the only thing that helped, but this disease just had to run its course and no fast cure was available.

At the same time as this outbreak, the farmers were losing hundreds of chickens from leucosis (a blood irregularity in birds). The pigeons may have had a form of this disease, but we will never know. The point is, you will find, through years of keeping pigeons, that many things will arise that cannot be explained. And this was just one of them.

Worms

Worms are one of the principal forms of parasitic life, and almost all forms of life can be infected by at least one type of worm. If you have ever kept a dog, you know the importance of worming. The pigeon is no exception and should be wormed at least 6 times a year. The reason worms are so hard to eliminate is that it is easy to kill the worm, but hard to break its life-cycle. The worm might be dead, but if the pigeon has access to its eggs, the cycle starts all over. Since the eggs are passed in the droppings and it is natural for a pigeon to eat almost anything, the risk of contamination by worms is constant. Good sanitation will help prevent the bird from ingesting the eggs. Following are the most common worms found in pigeons.

Roundworms

Roundworms (*Ascaridia columbae*) are the most common worms that trouble pigeons. The full-grown worm may be up to 2″ in length, and a female roundworm may lay as many as 10 million eggs in a lifetime. This worm lives in the intestine of the pigeon and feeds off the digested food.

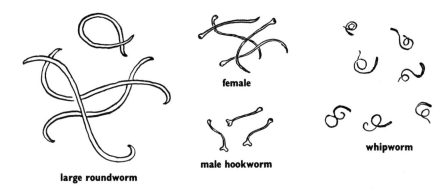

female

male hookworm

whipworm

large roundworm

Many parasitic invasions can be detected only by examining the pigeon droppings. This chart shows you three different kinds of worms to be on guard against.

On only rare occasions has a bird died from roundworms. The only apparent harm they do to pigeons is to make them sluggish and thus prevent them from performing well in the races. Many top flyers who had a bad year have found that their flyers were heavily infested with roundworms.

If you put piperazine citrate in the birds' drinking water for 48 hours, this will eliminate most of the roundworms. To prevent recurrence, you must keep your loft in top sanitary condition and give the birds no chance to pick up contaminated food.

Tapeworms

There are many species of tapeworms. *Apormia delafondi* (the "pigeon tapeworm") is the only one that infests pigeons. It lives in the small intestine and may grow to 7″ in length.

Every species of tapeworm requires an intermediate host to complete its life-cycle. The intermediate host (such as an insect) eats the eggs that are passed in droppings. Insects, the most common carrier, are then eaten by the pigeon and the pigeon is thus infected with the tapeworm. When the tapeworm hatches, the scolex (head) attaches itself to the intestines by sharp spines. The only symptom of tapeworm is that it makes the birds sluggish and thus unable to perform well in the races. In severe cases the pigeons have diarrhea and leg weakness. You may occasionally find tapeworm segments in their droppings or protruding from the pigeon's rectum.

There are a number of medications on the market that kill the segments, but none is capable of dislodging the head. If the bird is of little value, it is best to destroy it. A valuable pigeon is always worth trying to save, and if one of your best flyers becomes infested with tapeworm, you can at least keep the tapeworm's growth under control with one of the tapeworm remedies on the market. However, if you find that this bird's performance is hindered by the tapeworm infestation, you should destroy it, too.

The best course of action to take in dealing with tapeworms is prevention: Keep the pigeon droppings cleaned up and do not let feed contaminated by droppings lie about your loft.

Hairworms

The hairworm (*Capillaria columbae*) is another frequent parasite on the pigeon. These worms can cause much damage, and in severe cases death often occurs. Heavily infested pigeons have diarrhea, are droopy and lose all interest in eating and drinking. Just-weaned youngsters seem to be most susceptible.

These worms can be detected only by examining the birds' droppings under a microscope and looking for the eggs. Hairworms live only 7 months, and if the bird has not eaten any worm eggs he will be completely free from hairworms. There is no known medication to give pigeons to rid them of these worms. If the loft is bright and dry, the eggs will die, for only dampness keeps them alive until they can be eaten by their new host.

Roundworms, tapeworms, and hairworms are the three most frequent worms found in pigeons. Listed below are a few of the lesser known worms.

1. Strongyle worm (*Ornithostrongylus quadriradiatus*). It is much on the order of the hairworm, but the afflicted pigeon's thirst increases and, although the appetite remains unaffected, there is much vomiting. The pigeon loses weight until death occurs. Use the same preventative measures as against hairworms.

2. Stomach-wall worm (*Dispharynx nasuta*). This worm attacks

the stomach walls and, like the tapeworm, it needs an intermediate host. Many different types of insects are the intermediate host. A cure is not known, and only prevention can eliminate these worms. Pigeons that come down with the incurable stomach-wall worm must be destroyed to protect the rest of your flock.

The following are rare in pigeons, but do occur: eye-worm (*Oxyspirura mansoui*), flukes (*trematodes*), *Tetrameres americana* (a form of roundworm), and cecal worm (*Heterdkis gallinae*). There may be many other forms of worms to be found in pigeons, but very little has been written about them. The worms previously discussed are the only ones of interest to the pigeon fancier.

Insects

Many different types of insects can infest the pigeon and its loft. No matter what type of insect is present, the fact is that insects may do damage and are always undesirable. The most dangerous insects are the ones that are parasitic. Most of them do damage in one way or another: some destroy feathers, others live off the pigeons' blood, and almost all are carriers of disease and worms.

Lice

There are five kinds of lice which infest pigeons, but there is no excuse for a bird to have lice because lice are easy to control. Lice are brown in color and have six legs. They live their entire life upon the pigeon, attaching their eggs to the pigeon's feathers. The female louse lays so many eggs that, theoretically, in 6 months one pair of lice may have a quarter of a million descendants. This is why you must be constantly on the watch for lice. Every time you handle a pigeon, take time to inspect some of the feathering to make sure no lice are present. Following are the five varieties that infest the pigeon.

1. The feather louse (*Columbicola columbae*) is the most common. It is long and slender and is very easily seen. It does not lodge in any specific location, but may be found on any part of the pigeon. This louse may do harm to feathers: very often it eats holes in the flights. The feather louse's diet consists of the skin scales and parts of feathers.

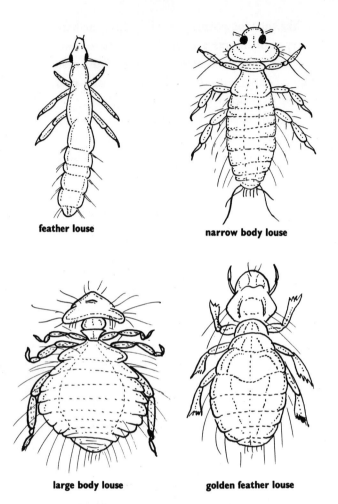

feather louse

narrow body louse

large body louse

golden feather louse

Low cost commercial products easily do away with all the lice shown in this chart. Although some types do less harm than others, all species of lice are potential disease-carriers—and only a careless fancier would allow them to torment his pigeons.

2. The little feather louse (*Coniodes damicornis*) is among the least frequently found of the five pigeon lice. It locates itself only in the feathers that are in front of the oil gland. The little feather louse seems to do very little damage, but its elimination is desirable.

3. The narrow body louse (*Colpocepholum turbinatum*) is the

rarest of pigeon lice, but this louse may damage your bird by sucking its blood. This species is found mostly in the warmer, damp climates.

4. The large body louse (*Menacanthus latus*) is the largest known pigeon louse. It is found on the skin near the base of the pigeon's rump, near the vent, or near the base of large flight or tail feathers. Instead of being brown, it is yellow in color and lives off the blood of the pigeon. It gets most of its nourishment by puncturing a pin-feather that is filled with blood.

5. The golden feather louse (*Goniocotes bidentatus*) is just as common as the feather louse and it can be found at the base of the body feathers. It is much shorter and thicker than the feather louse and gets its name from its golden color. It does not suck blood, but is constantly moving about and causing great discomfort to the pigeon.

Although lice cause no great harm, you should always examine your birds for them. A louse-infested pigeon is nervous and cannot sleep because the lice are moving about on its body.

There are many different kinds of products on the market which will completely free your loft of lice. They are low in cost and easy to apply. There are various powders that may be applied directly to the pigeon, or you may buy a kind that you make into a mixture and then paint the loft walls and perches with it. There are different brands of roost paints that also do the job. The Vapona Insecticide strip not only kills flies and insects but also eliminates lice. Sodium fluoride is another chemical that completely eliminates all species of lice. Always remember that there is no excuse for having lice present in your loft. These lice preventatives are also effective in eliminating other types of insects.

Mites

Mites cause more misery and discomfort than lice. All mites are very tiny, have 8 legs, and live off the host's blood. They live in the cracks and crevices of the loft and come out only at night, to feed upon the pigeons' blood. At night you can hear the birds moving about: stamping their feet as if they were dancing. If you turn a light on, you will see little red specks scurrying back to safety.

Birds from an infected loft sit with ruffled feathers and continuously scratch and pick. Because the mite lives on blood, the bird most often suffers from anemia and is lazy and unwilling to fly. Do not expect to win races if mites are present in your loft.

Mites are hard to eliminate. Lice preventatives do not always work in killing mites, so you must purchase a commercial mixture made exclusively for eliminating mites. In all matters concerning pigeons, you should practice *prevention*. Do not wait until sickness or parasites enter your loft. Following is a list of the mites that are most common to the pigeon.

1. Red mite (*Dermanyssus gallinae*)
2. Feather mite (*Falculifer rostratus*)
3. Feather mite (*Megninia columbae*)
4. Scaly-leg mite (*Nemidocoptes mutans*)
5. Flesh mite (*Laminosiptes cysticola*)
6. Depluming scabies (*Cnemidocoptes gallinae*): The depluming scabies is an itch mite that lives at the base of the feather and eats the feather so that it breaks off at skin level. This is often known as FEATHER ROT. You eliminate this pest with the same means you use to get rid of regular mites, but there is also a commercial feather-rot cream on the market that will heal birds that have been tormented by this mite.
7. Air-sac mite (*Cytolerichus nudus*): This mite lives in the respiratory system of the pigeon. The symptoms are a droopy appearance, much coughing, and the bird's being unable to fly for a length of time. Diagnosis can be made only by finding eggs in the droppings or by dissecting a pigeon. There is no known cure, and the infested bird should be destroyed.

The Mosquito

All pigeon fanciers agree that the mosquito is a nuisance, but few realize the damage that mosquitoes can do. Mosquitoes are the main source in the spreading of pigeon pox, and if large swarms of mosquitoes invade the loft, there is certain to be anemia among the birds. Pigeons that are being attacked by mosquitoes very seldom get a good night's sleep, and this throws them out of racing condition. When entering the loft at night you can hear them stamping their feet trying to rid themselves of the mosquitoes.

Many diseases besides pigeon pox are carried by the mosquito. This is reason enough to try to prevent them from entering the loft. Use screens at night. Carbola, a medicated whitewash, is the best deterrent in mosquito prevention, and the Vapona Insecticide strip is also very effective.

Keep in mind that all forms of insects and parasites may be dangerous and they are not welcome in the loft.

Garden Precautions

In feeding cabbage be sure that the vegetable is clean and healthy. Cabbage may carry a mould disease called club-root. If pigeons are fed cabbage infected with club-root, this will put them out of racing form. There is always a risk in feeding any type of food (including all greens). To reduce this risk, always make sure that all food is of the highest quality and that the greens are fresh. Thoroughly wash all greens before feeding.

Clover is another possible danger, and therefore the flyer would be wise to keep it out of his lawn. If you allow clover to grow in your lawn and the pigeon eats it, your bird will be thrown out of racing form.

Garden snails should also be eliminated from the fancier's garden because birds that peck or eat empty snail shells may pick up the liver fluke—and this is lethal.

18. THE OFF SEASON

It seems that the off season would bring hours of rest and relaxation to the fancier, but this is not true. It is only in the off season that you can take care of items that lack of time made it impossible for you to attend to during the racing season. This is the time for painting and fixing the loft. The off season also allows you time to paint the nests and perches or fix anything that you had to neglect during the racing season. At this time you should completely scrub and disinfect the inside of the loft. During breeding and racing times, these chores could not be taken care of because of lack of time and also because they disturb the birds too much.

Culling

The time when you are separating the birds by sexes (usually mid-summer) is the best time to go through the loft and weed out the birds that are not up to standard.

Remember that when you purchased the birds, you wanted only the best. Keep this in mind when culling and do not sell or give away birds that are below standard. You must harden your heart and kill them. You are not doing another fancier any favor by giving him inferior pigeons with hopes that they may become champion stock-birds. If they are not good enough for you they will not be good enough for anybody else. If you desire to give pigeons away to friends, it is advisable to give them late hatches out of your very best. Many late hatches have developed into champion breeders.

Pedigrees and Records

The cold winter months are the best time to bring your flying and breeding records up to date. Make notes on every bird that you bred, how *all* your birds flew, whether they trapped well or not, which ones were lost or killed, and any other information of importance. Do not rely on your memory because next year you will have forgotten most of these important data.

The winter is also a good time to make out pedigrees on birds you gave away and on any new birds that you acquired. Make as many notes as possible on the pedigrees and bring the race results up to date. A pedigree loses its importance if the race results of the youngsters are not noted. A pedigree with 20 generations is useless unless there are winners connected to it. Every racing-pigeon-man is more interested in the victories than in the ancestors.

Reading

The winter is an ideal time to catch up on your reading. If you are not on the top of the heap, then there is much to learn and you may learn through reading and trying out what you read. When reading you might find the one thing that will change you from being only a fair flyer to one of the best. Very often fanciers are close to becoming a success, but they continuously make the same few mistakes. Through reading, you may realize these mistakes, and just a little change may be all you need.

Another winter job is to plan on paper next year's matings. Pairs can be mated and re-mated on paper until you arrive at the correct matings. This also gives you time to compare ancestors and plan on certain inbred pairs to help strengthen your stock.

You should also plan any changes that you desire to make. Do not wait until the racing season to make plans because then they are usually done in haste.

NEST - 6 - Breeder - PAIR - 2   NEST - 6 - Breeder - PAIR - 2

AU-63-FHM-639   AU-66-B-8475   639 - NOTES - 8475
BLUE BAR COCK   BLUE-CHECK-HEN

Color	Band No.	Laid	Cup	Hatch
Blue B	AU-69-B-724	3/5	On 3/7 Time	3/24
Blue B	AU-69-B-725	3/7		3/24
BlueCk	AU-69-B-745	4/14	On 4/16 Time	5/2
Blue B	WFCT. " " 746			
Bk. B	AU-69-B-764	5/23	On 5/25 Time	6/10
Bk. B	AU-69-B-765	6/28	On 6/30 Time	

gave eggs to STERNER 7/1/69

765 - gave to JIM GALLAGHER
764 - " " ANDY BIASKO
725 - " " BIGGY

HAVING A LITTLE TROUBLE WITH THIS PAIR, EVEN THOUGH SHE MATES WITH 639 WHEN RELEASED SHE TRYS TO GO BACK TO HER OLD NEST.

3/4/69 ON CHECKING 8475 FOUND HER TO BE VERY FAT ON HANDLING SHE GASPS FOR AIR. HER VENTS ARE OPEN, BUT MUCH FAT BETWEEN THE VENT. SHE GIVES ME THE IMPRESSION OF BEING EGG BOUND.

8475 TOOK 14 DAYS TO LAY, (AGT YEAR SHE TOOK 19 DAYS) TO LAY.
639 EXCEP. GOOD ON THE NEST.

A typical page from E. C. Welty's record-book, breeders' section. If you do not have time all-year-round to keep records as thorough as this, the off season is an ideal time to catch up on your paper work.

Activities

Most of the club and combine meetings are held during the off season. It is your duty to stay in good standing with the club by attending these meetings, placing your vote in the election of officers, and voicing your opinion on matters that have been questionable during the year. Only at the meetings does your opinion count, and any complaining done outside the club is nothing but idle talk.

Also during the off season there are conventions, banquets, and parties to attend. These functions are a very important part of pigeon racing and they allow the wives to participate. If at all possible attend them because many good times and friendships have developed from them.

Shows have become the biggest winter activity and they are so important that a chapter has been devoted to the hows and whys of showing pigeons.

19. PIGEON SHOWS

The showing of racing pigeons once was just a sideline of many racing lofts, but now is very popular and many people who do not race any more just show their birds. It has gotten to the point where showing-competition is just as intense as racing.

It is just as much of a victory to win in the shows as it is to win a race. Your entries must be in first-class condition to win top prizes in shows. The planning and the skill required are just as exacting as in winning a race. To be a successful showman, you not only have to produce birds of the show-standard, but you must also learn to have a great deal of patience and determination.

A well-conditioned show bird is really a joy to behold! It should have just completed a perfect moult, and its new coat of feathers glows with quality, color, and health. If you have taken good care of your pigeons for the entire year, you have already made the proper steps for entering your birds in a show.

Here is how to pick and prepare birds for the shows and also what the judges look for when judging: If you have taken good care of your birds and put them through a good moult, you know that somewhere in your loft is a future ribbon-winner. Make sure that your pigeons continue to receive their weekly bath and make especially sure that their last bath is 4 days before the show. These 4 days give them a chance to regain the oil in their feathers.

Spend as much time as possible with your birds, always talking to them, touching them, handling them and restoring their faith in you as a gentle, loving owner. The importance of this is to tame your birds, as some may have a tendency to become a little wild after the moult and those winter months when you spend less time with your birds than during the rest of the year. Many beautiful pigeons have been thrown out of competition because of their wildness. To realize the importance of this, you ought to be aware of what happened at the 1959 South Hills Pigeon

IF 67 HPC 1642 Blue Bar White Flight has won "Best in Show" plus two firsts and other diplomas. She is a Havenith-Huysken Van Riel cross with the yellow eye. Retired from racing, she is now a stock-bird and has already bred three winners.

Proportion is the key word in selecting birds for show-competition. Here, Belge 58 6062040, a blue-check hen of Havenith strain with the yellow eye.

Show: the four judges were deadlocked on which bird deserved the title of *Best in Show*. After much contemplation, the judges went back to the judging cages to look for some fault that would eliminate one of the two finalists. Whenever the judges went to catch a beautiful blue-checkered hen, she jumped all over the cage trying to elude the judge. When the judge went to handle a blue-checkered cock, he went right over and began fighting with the judge's hand. This tameness was the final factor in deciding the *Best in Show*.

Each judge looks for the same thing, but each one has different points that he feels are more important. Your birds should not be overly fat. This is a sure way to get them eliminated from competition. The next thing that should come under consideration is the bird's general appearance. The Racing Pigeon should suggest health, strength, intelligence, alertness and perfect balance. All parts of the pigeon should be in complete proportion to one another. It should stand well on its feet, with its legs being set apart and neither too straight nor too short or too long. Also, the legs should be free of feathers from the hock down.

The bird should not be too large nor too small, but should be of medium build, with the head, body, wings, legs and tail being in correct proportion to one another. Also, it is best if your bird, when standing, looks as though it is ready to fly and stands at a 40- or 50-degree angle.

Your bird's eyes should be bright, clean and alert and should be placed well back in the head with the mid-line of the beak pointing towards the center of the eye. The eye color is not too important, just so the iris is a bright color with very strong pigmentation. It is also preferable that the eye cere completely encircle the eye.

The head and neck should show strength, be well developed, and be a clear indicator of sex. The beak should be strong, even, and not too long. The eye cere and wattle should be smooth without any undue coarseness. The neck should be smooth without any frills or marks and it should run smoothly into the body, giving the impression that the neck and body are one.

The body shape is not always important, just so it is in proportion to the rest of the pigeon. The breast-bone or "keel" should be straight, strong, thick, and not too deep. Its length should be neither too short nor too long in proportion to the bird's whole build. The vents should be located right at the end of the breast-bone. These are one of the top indicators of the strength and health of the pigeon. The vents should be strong, close together, and lie up into the body. Whenever a pigeon has a good, strong vent, the rest of the skeleton structure is just as strong. You must remember that the vent-bone helps sustain the bird's internal organs during flight.

The back should be broad, strong, flat, and give the impression of power and strength. The back should not give under pressure when being held. The rump should be firm and smooth and have plenty of feathers. It should run smoothly into the tail, again giving you the impression of being one.

The wings should also be in complete proportion to the rest of the body. When the bird is standing, the tips of its wings should not come more than 1″ from the end of the tail. When the wings are extended as if in flight, the primary and secondary flights on each wing should run together as if they were one piece, without any gaps between them. Each wing should also have plenty of feathers on the underside. The wings should, moreover, be free of fret marks, pin-holes (louse-borings), and any other marks that would go against them in show-competition.

The tail should be medium in length, with broad feathers, and should be free of defects. When the bird is standing or being held, the tail feathers should fold together, giving the impression that they are one feather. The feathering, viewed as a whole,

All four of these racing pigeons are show-competition winners (from the loft of E. C. Welty).

should be firm, thick, soft, and closely overlapped, giving the over-all impression of being painted on. The bird should have strong, supple muscles that give the impression of strength to whoever holds it.

After you find a few birds in your loft with the above qualities, it is now time to prepare them for the shows. It is best to wash the birds' feet and, with a pair of tweezers, pull out the few feathers that are on the legs. Then, with a damp cloth, gently wipe the bird clean of any dirt that would take away from its beauty. When you have completed this, place your show birds into the pigeon crate, making sure that they are separated with dividers to keep them from fighting. Many birds have been eliminated from competition just because of damage done by last-minute fighting.

If your birds have all these qualities, you have a good chance of placing and even going on to win *Best in Show*. After all these things have been taken into consideration, it still comes down to what the judges prefer. It may be the color, the eye, or any one of a number of things that is the deciding factor in whether you win or lose—but remember one thing: Your bird must be healthy. The secret of being a great pigeon-man is knowing how to maintain a healthy loft of pigeons.

GLOSSARY OF MOST-OFTEN-USED TERMS

Air-sacs: Nine hollow areas within the pigeon's body which contain air.

Apple head: A high or bulging forehead.

Back skull: The back portion of the head.

Bananas: The pattern of the scales on the feet and legs.

Banded: A pigeon that carries a band on his leg is called "banded."

Bar: The colored band located at the base of the tail.

Barren hen: A hen that cannot lay eggs.

Bars: The two or three bands of color which are located at the back part of the wing.

Bastard flight: A small flightlike feather that is found at the joint of the wing butt.

Beak angle: Angle of beak in relation to the head.

Beard: A pigeon with excess flesh and feathers directly under the lower beak is said to "have a beard."

Bib: Color pattern of the front part of the neck.

Billing: A process in courtship (pigeon kissing).

Blocky: Broad and short of body; also called "apple-bodied" or "cobby."

Bolting eye: A very prominent eye.

Breast: Crop area of the body; also includes the front muscles.

Broad: A pigeon wide in the chest is said to be "broad."

Broken eye: Irises of two colors.

Brooding: Sitting on eggs.

Bulleye: A very dark colored eye.

Candy: A mixture of small grains used as a treat.

Cere: Flesh surrounding the eye.

Checker: A color pattern of the wing.

Cheeks: The puffy areas directly below the eyes.

Clutches: The name given to the set of eggs laid.

Coopies: (chicos) Birds used in bringing down race birds.

Corkiness: The description given to a pigeon that is light in weight and in race condition.

Coverts: The small feathers that cover the flights and thus protect them from the elements.

Crop or craw: A fleshy pocket for storing feed.

Crest: Reversed feathers on the back of the head as in the Satinette.

Crooked keel: A crooked breast-bone; very undesirable in racing pigeons, as it shows lack of stamina.

Crown: Top of head.

Cull: To eliminate unwanted pigeons.

Deep: A bird that is deep or large in the breast-bone.

Down: Yellowish covering found on newly hatched pigeons.

Egg-bound: A hen that is unable to lay a completely formed egg.

Eye-sign: A theory that connects different types of eyes to racing and breeding ability.

Face: The front part of the head, from the eyes forward.

Flagging: Forcing pigeons to fly for a certain length of time; it usually involves keeping them up by the use of a flag.

Flight cage: Wire cage that fits on landing board, used to break in youngsters.

Flights: The 20 long feathers on the wing.

Floaters: A pigeon that spends much time floating in the air instead of flying hard.

Form: Condition, used in describing race birds.

Fret marks: Any mark or deformity on the feathers.

Frill: Feathers on the front of the neck that form a frill-like pattern.

Gape: Size of mouth opening.

Girth: Circumference of the body.

Gullet: Fleshy fold under the beak—same as in bearded.

Hackle: The brightly colored neck feathers.

Inbreeding: Breeding of closely related pigeons.

Jewing: The part of the wattle on the lower beak.

Keel: Breast-bone.

Knee: Hock.

Late hatch: Name given to third or fourth hatches.

Mandible: Beak or bill.

Moult: The process of growing new feathers.

Naked: Poorly feathered.

Natural system: Flying birds that are kept paired: sitting on eggs or rearing youngsters.

Nicking: Term used when a strain or family of pigeons cross well and produce winners.

Open-loft: Leaving the traps open so that the birds come and go as they please; also called "free bobbing."

Overfly: A loft located farther from the release-point than another loft is said to have "overfly" on the loft with the shorter distance.

Pectorals: The muscles lying on both sides of the keel.

Pied: A pigeon with one or more white flights in a wing is called "pied" or a "white-flight."

Pigment: Coloring of iris.

Pin-feathers: Name given to feathers that have not yet broken through the shaft.

Pinched: If the area between the eye and wattle is narrow, it is said that the pigeon's face is "pinched."

Pipping: The chipping of the egg during hatching.

Plume: Name given to the quality of feathers.

Pot eggs: Wooden or glass eggs used to replace real eggs when hatching is undesirable—they are used a great deal in old-bird flying.

Preening: To trim or dress the feathers with the beak.

Primaries: The 10 large outer wing-flights.

Prisoners: Pigeons unable to be released because they do not stay at your loft.

Pumping: Feeding of the youngsters by the parents.

Rank: A process in courtship when the hen is thoroughly aroused and is eager to tread with the cock.

Rump: The heavily feathered area at the lower part of the back.

Runt: A youngster that did not develop properly.

Scales: The dead skin on the body which surrounds the breast-bone.

Secondaries: The 10 smaller flight feathers, closest to the body.

Shallow: When the muscles along the breast-bone are not very staple and the body gives the feeling of sharpness, this is called being "shallow."

Silky: Healthy feathering.

Skimmie: Common street-pigeon.

Splash: Any colored pigeon that has areas of white splashed about.

Split tail: Tail with a gap in its middle.

Squab: A young pigeon from 1 to 30 days of age.

Squeaker: A young pigeon just learning to eat.

Stall trap: A trap designed so that only one pigeon may enter at a time; moreover, it has a locking device that keeps the bird in the stall until the countermark is removed: only after the fancier opens a release may the pigeon enter the loft.

Stockings: Feathers on legs and feet.

Stunted: Same as runt.

Throwback: A color-pattern or type that does not look like either parent, but which greatly resembles a distant relative.

Ticked: One or two white feathers found on the head or face.

Tits: A small portion of the wattle which has grown on both sides of the lower beak.

Toe nails: Claws.

Top skull: Top of head.

Treading: The sexual act.

Tripping: The term given to young birds' activity when they leave the immediate area of the loft and fly for long periods of time.

Vent bones: Two small bones directly behind the breast-bone.
Washed out: A pigeon with bad eye color.
Wattle: Flesh found on top and bottom of beak.
Weaning: Taking the young away from their parents.
Widowhood: A racing system flown without hens.
Wing butt: The part of the wing that is most forward when closed; this is found at the joint of the hand and forearm.
Yearling: A 1-year-old pigeon.

Suggested Readings on Widowhood Flying

Depauw, *The Widowhood System within Every Fancier's Reach.* (D. Van Keerverghen & Sons, Brussels).

Gordon, *Practical Widowhood.* (Published by *Racing Pigeon Bulletin*).

Langstone, *Winning Ways with Widowers.* (Racing Pigeon Publishing Co., Ltd., 19 Doughty Street, London, Nov. 1954).

Index